Becoming One Flesh

BECOMING
ONE
FLESH

Growth in Christian Marriage

Denise Lardner Carmody

John Tully Carmody

THE UPPER ROOM
Nashville, Tennessee

Becoming One Flesh

Copyright © 1984 by The Upper Room. All rights reserved.

Scripture quotations not otherwise identified are from the Revised Standard Version of the Bible, copyrighted 1946, 1952, and © 1971 by the Division of Christian Education, National Council of the Churches of Christ in the United States of America, and are used by permission.

Scripture quotations designated AP are the authors' paraphrase.

Excerpts from *The Ants of God* by W.T. Tyler, copyright © 1981 by W.T. Tyler, are reprinted by permission of Doubleday & Company, Inc.

Excerpts from *Morgan's Passing* by Anne Tyler, copyright © 1980 by Anne Tyler Modarressi, are reprinted by permission of Alfred A. Knopf, Inc. and Russel & Volkening, Inc.

Excerpt from *Dale Loves Sophie to Death* by Robb Forman Dew, copyright © 1979, 1981 by Robb Forman Dew, is reprinted by permission of Farrar, Straus & Giroux, Inc. and Penguin Books.

Selected lines from *Your Word Is Near* by Huub Oosterhuis are reprinted by permission of Paulist Press.

Book Design: Harriette Bateman
First Printing: November, 1984 (5)
Library of Congress Catalog Card Number: 84-50841
ISBN 0-8358-0486-0

Printed in the United States of America

FOR
Joe and Joann Corlett

Contents

Preface

THIS LITTLE BOOK summarizes thoughts of the early morning and late night about Christian marriage. The thoughts are holistic rather than systematic, spun off from the mysterious center of Christian faith rather than marshaled inexorably to fit some system. We hope they will receive the bit of silence and touch of hospitable prayer necessary for their flowering. Then, whatever their smudges and flaws, the Spirit will be able to make them profitable.

How might such profit appear? In the common ways that both love and Christian maturation show themselves. From silence and the touch of the Spirit we may occasionally feel reconverted, healed, put back together. What was disordered and troubled may gain peace. What was confused may heed once again its better calling. The pastoral impulse behind any book such as this is the flourishing of its readers in prayer and service. If anything we say helps couples deepen their trust in God, their openness to one another, and their service in their communities, we will be more than satisfied.

Readers who think they recognize themselves in the positive examples we offer may take an extra dessert. Readers who think they recognize themselves in our negative examples may assure themselves we are writing fiction.

Our thanks to Janice Grana and Rueben Job of The Upper Room for initiating the project; to Joann Wolski Conn and Walter Conn for bibliographic leads on religious development (and good marital example); and to Karla Kraft for her usual high standard of manuscript preparation.

CHAPTER

— 1 —

Introduction

The Goodness of Creation

"IN THE BEGINNING God created the heavens and the earth." That is the first line of the Christian Bible (Gen. 1:1), something most people in our culture have heard a dozen times. Fewer people have heard, in a way that has seeped into their marrow, the line that punctuates the rest of the creation account: "God saw that it was good" (Gen. 1:10, 12). As a result, fewer people see creation as faith says it is: a cornucopia of blessings, a profusion of divine gifts. Indeed, their failure to appreciate the goodness of creation leads many people to question that God is the world's source. Not being sure that the world is good, many people think creation may have been haphazard, accidental, without meaning or plan.

In the beginning of a reflection on marriage, such negative thoughts can be ruinous. If we doubt the meaningfulness of the world, the worth of the stars in the heavens or the grains of sand along the sea, how shall we treasure the promise to Abraham that his progeny would be as numerous as the stars in the heavens and the grains of sand along the sea (Gen. 13:17)? How shall we treasure Christ, who is a new creation, or the church, which Christ married to bring myriad offspring to God? A first word, then, about the goodness of creation, to get our reflections on Christian marriage started correctly.

It is early September, a good time where we live. The furnace of high summer shows its first signs of shutting off. The little kids trudge back to school, relieved that someone else will plan their next days. In the parks and pools that the kids have abandoned adults stroll, swim, and sigh with relief. A new cycle is beginning, a new year of study getting under way. From the dazzling blue sky the Creator seems to promise that it can be a good year, if we wish. At some ultimate level, all is right with the world.

That is the message of earliest morning, when we creep out to rescue the newspaper. In the kitchen, as the coffee perks, the newspaper challenges this message brutally. The Soviets have killed more than 250 people because a Korean commercial airliner wandered into Soviet airspace. A prominent United States senator has died of a massive heart attack. Violence and greed smudge the side columns. At the beginning of many days, the newspaper creates confusion and depression. Looking upon this creation, many readers think the world is very bad. The hopefulness of Genesis and Jesus seems terribly naive. Let there be the light of the news, a revelation of the past twenty-four hours, and faith can seem futile.

So the two voices of conscience, the hopeful and the depressing, launch many of our days in confusion. Rosy-fingered dawn prompts us to thank God for the light of our eyes and the air we breathe. Lurid headlines prompt us to stop our mouths, shade our eyes, taste for acid rain. Each voice has its data, its logic, its wisdom. The goodness of creation is not the whole story, nor is the depravity of the worst news. As we mature, life increasingly shows itself a matter of both/and, not either/or. In the beginning of any serious religious reflection lies the traditional wisdom that the whole of things is greater than we. We are the pots, not the potter. Genesis and Jesus take us beyond what is certain or obvious, into the depths of the real God's mystery.

Creation is only good because of the depths of the real God's mystery. There is no sure goodness in the creation of a false God, a less than ultimate mystery. The lilies of the field do not overbalance the patients in the cancer wards. It is not obvious that the saints outweigh the assassins. Any vision in which creation is very good depends on eyes of faith. Only those who find God a light too bright for human comprehension convincingly say that the light has shone in the darkness and the darkness never overcome it. Only those who have wept at Christ's cross feel, with the full surprise of joy, that suffering and death are not ultimate. As Proverbs 1:7 says, the beginning of wisdom is the fear of the Lord, the realization that without our Creator we are utterly bereft. The beginning of any useful consideration of marriage is the realization that graces of the Creator such as marriage never are cheap.

God did make the heavens and the earth in the beginning. Each moment in the existence of any creature does depend upon God's quickening love. The beauties of rosy-fingered dawn are not misleading. The horrors of the headlines only magnify our need for faith. Yet we cannot in good conscience make any of these assertions casually, lazily, unreflectively. Each puts forth an astounding claim: The goodness of creation depends on the gratuitous love of a mystery we must accept in faith.

The Goodness of Marriage

In Genesis, Hosea, the Song of Songs, Ephesians, and other books, the Bible lays out a positive view of marriage. Overall, it has no question that the sharing of man and woman or the procreation of children is very good. To be sure, some texts reflect a sour view of women and children. Not everything from the biblical authors' pens is sweet and light, profound and faith-filled. But of the essential thrust there can be no doubt: God made humanity male-female; for reason of their mutual attraction, the sexes rightly leave father and mother and cleave to one another; the church is to Christ as a bride to her husband; heaven rejoices at the nuptials of the Lamb. Any serious questions about the goodness of marriage, therefore, lie in the areas of postbiblical Christian history or faithless interpretations of daily experience.

In the centuries after the New Testament, many prominent church leaders did on occasion deprecate marriage. Led astray by their zeal for celibacy, such church fathers as Tertullian, Jerome, Augustine, and Chrysostom wrote things about women and marriage that curl the sensitive ear.[1] But neither these writers, nor their imitators in later centuries, ever took the church catholic away from the central biblical assertion that marriage is an obvious part of God's holy plan. Indeed, when Manicheans or Albigensians denied the goodness of marriage, the mainstream church branded them heretical. At the Protestant Reformation, a return to biblical sources brought a renewed assertion that marriage and the lay state are good in the eyes of God, the normal Christian vocation. Against the tendencies of monks and celibate clergy to exalt virginity, Luther, Calvin, and other leading reformers argued for the clear biblical assumption that most sanctity would occur in marriage and the world.

Still, accepting the biblical assumption of the goodness of marriage, and tying it fast to the living mystery of the real God, has been no easier in this case than regarding creation as a whole. One does not have to live two decades to learn that many marriages are combat zones. By the time one has lived five decades it is clear that marriage has been seared by Satan, as well as blessed by God. Nowadays, when the number of people divorcing threatens to outnumber the people remaining together, only those with their heads in the sand sing the glories of marriage unselfconsciously. For the many reasons that sociologists can bring forward, and the deeper reasons that faith senses to be at work, young people today find it hard to marry confidently, deeply fear that their teeth, too, will soon be on edge.

We saw this fear realized recently in one of our students. Married little more than a year, he was shattered to hear his wife say she wanted out—all the more so since she could give him no reasons, no specific complaints, only "It isn't working for me. I'm not happy." In retrospect, these two young people in their early twenties probably married with unrealistic, even giddy expectations. Their wedding ceremony made more of balloons and flowers, candles and folk music, than of solid scripture and sacrament. But clearly they had been in love, been bright, been aware of the cultural obstacles to marital success. What went wrong, that they shipwrecked so quickly? How could something supposed to be very good have aborted or become tainted in a year?

These questions are not very different than the questions middle-aged people ask themselves, when they hear friends married twenty years declare they are calling it quits. Some of the patterns are obvious—for example, the tendency of forty-year-olds to fling off with a younger playmate. Other patterns are strange, hidden deep in sufferings one or both spouses have long kept to themselves. The counselor has to go case by case, blending hard realism with gentle sympathy. Loves do die. Mistakes do beg correction. In the dark silence of deep prayer to God, many preconceptions do fall away. Still, when all is said and done, a lot of hurt and wreckage awaits explanation. Betrayals of intimacy, neglect of kids, guilts and recriminations knock steadily at the answer man's door. Too many people supposed to be beloved in Christ are dragging themselves to neutral corners, bloodied and abused. If marriage is so good, why are so many marriages so bad?

Our first answer has to be oblique. In the eyes of faith, most of us don't do the good we should, do do some evil we should not. In the eyes of faith, we suffer many problems because we close ourselves to the deepest sources of guidance and healing, the ministrations of the Spirit. One can say this simplistically, as a substitute for hard thinking, or one can say it profoundly, at the depths where the Spirit groans in prayer. At the depths, our sinfulness is both accusing and redeemable. Our closures are accusing, because we see how they deny our creaturehood, fundamentally reject our faith. But they are also redeemable, because the Spirit groaning in our depths is the spirit of Christ, who has overcome the world. Even when our hearts condemn us, "God is greater than our hearts" (1 John 3:20). Only the love of the God greater than our hearts makes marriage solidly good—surely stronger than its enemies—just as only that love makes there be a creation at all.

The Necessity of Growth

God is our rock and salvation—that is the theme we are playing. Brains are fine, effort is important, but neither guarantees the goodness of marriage. As with our conviction about the goodness of creation, our conviction about the goodness of marriage is terribly vulnerable until we rivet it onto the mystery of God. This is standard enough theology, front and center in any orthodox explanation of grace. But it only becomes our personal faith when we have clearly seen the frailty of the alternatives. People who think that high spirits or sex appeal or a common love of children or a common hustle for money will make them a first-rate marriage badly delude themselves. First-rate marriages evolve slowly and make large demands. They are so directly a function of the partners' overall growth that either partner's settling down in complacency, refusing to go deeper and wider, virtually closes the possibility. Good marriages have their sustaining joys, of course, and their moments of unexpectable grace. But these seldom announce themselves ahead of time, are not printed on any schedule. The airlines tell you when you will have snack or luncheon. The marital contract leaves blank both the feasts and the famines.

In the famous account of Moses' encounter with God at the burning bush, the name that Moses wrests from God is tantalizingly obscure. One of the best translations is, "I am as I shall be with you" (Exod. 3:14). Instead of giving Moses something lofty or philosophic ("The Almighty,"

"The Light Beyond All Light"), God promises an adventure: You'll find out by sojourning with me, sharing time, letting our relation unfold. Biblical faith is something historical (the story of a relation), something compelled to grow. It is something marital: sharing good times and bad, walking into the future side by side.

Such a faith can hasten to the aid of many troubled marriages. Because it is dynamic, changing, it can succor a relation that must keep generating the energies of growth. Just as baptism or confirmation does not settle one's business with God once and for all, so the marriage ceremony does not settle the spouses' business. It is only a beginning, phase one. The reality begun is a process rather than an unchanging connection. The partners are not two blocks joined in cement on a given day and hour. They are two personalities at the beginning of a process of overlapping, coinciding, becoming more individual by serving a common cause. Their best chance of retaining the communion they feel midst the euphoria and grace of the marriage ceremony lies in pushing it, pulling it, working it, letting it float. Day by day, sharing experience can bind them in cords that free them from loneliness, tame worries, and break down doubts. If they wish, they can become tough enough to expose more and more tender tissue, insightful enough to sense more and more mystery, faithful enough to endure the doldrums that are inevitable.

In the mystery of a God who would espouse him-or-herself to human beings, marriage takes on most of the paradoxes and potentialities of individual human growth. As Robert Kegan recently has shown with both fine scholarship and artful prose,[2] the human self ever needs to evolve. Ongoing growth (into fuller and deeper meaning) is our inmost law. The same seems to be the case with Christian marriage. The horizon in which it is most itself is a horizon of evolutionary change. Together, wife and husband share the fate of all living things, our common condemnation to aging. When they do this gracefully, supported by the helps of the Spirit, we speak of the maturation of their marriage. When they kick against the goad, refusing to be taught what to hold onto and what to let go, we speak of an unpeaceable kingdom, a castle no longer a home.

We know several couples who, quite unselfconsciously, furnish wonderful models of maturation. Two that now come to mind are striking because they stand at different stages in their life cycles. The younger couple have just had their third child, who probably will complete their family. Approaching their midthirties, they do their best to juggle two careers and fully shared parenting. Like no other couple we know, their chief delight is their children. Where other couples endure their kids on bad days and enjoy them when the fates are kind, this couple instinctively arrange work, play, study, and all the rest as functions of their parenting. It is not so much something they choose as something they are. They still get harried and grouchy. Many worries and questions remain. But right now they are head over heels in love through their children. Their main responsibility right now seems precisely the richest food for their own nurture. May they appreciate the rare measure of their blessing.

The older couple are nearing retirement and delighting in their first grandchildren. Around them the aura is not immersion in fruits of their union but freedom beyond the wars. So they seem to enjoy one another with a special gratitude. They have shared so much that, as death becomes a lengthening shadow, this time of peace seems a biblical measure, pressed down and overflowing. They are mature, ripe, fully grown. More than they know, they inspire many who are still callow.

The Possibility of Growth

Reflecting on the wonders of grace, God's unexpectable profusions of love, we might coin the axiom: What is necessary must be possible. What God commands, even seriously invites, God must make possible. In terms of general faith, this means that if we must learn who God is over time, by the ways that God chooses to be with us, we can so learn. Moreover, if it is possible to become increasingly intimate with the divine mystery, there should be people around who manifest such intimacy. And so there are: the people we call saints, the profoundly peaceful. Moving to the subject of marriage, if growth is the ground-level imperative, growth must be possible and we may expect mature married people to dot the scene. And so they do: people like our older couple, who are taping down the corners, wrapping round the bow; people like an old New Mexican couple that psychiatrist Robert Coles described a decade ago.

From his conversations with the wife, Coles composed the following reflection:

> A few drops of rain and I [the wife] feel grateful; the air is so fresh afterwards. I love to sit in the sun. We have the sun so often here, a regular visitor, a friend one can expect to see often and trust. I like to make tea for my husband and me. At midday we take our tea outside and sit on our bench, our backs against the wall of the house. Neither of us wants pillows; I tell my daughters and sons that they are soft—those beach chairs of theirs. Imagine beach chairs here in New Mexico, so far from any ocean! The bench feels strong to us, not uncomfortable. The tea warms us inside, the sun on the outside. I joke with my husband; I say we are part of the house; the adobe gets baked, and so do we. For the most part we say nothing, though. It is enough to sit and be part of God's world. We hear the birds talking to each other, and are grateful they come as close to us as they do; all the more reason to keep our tongues still and hold ourselves in one place.[3]

Here are a couple who seem instructively mature. They know how to be together in the world. They share a perspective on the world that makes them strong and religious. They know there is a time to work and a time to rest, a time to speak and a time to be silent. No doubt their traditional culture made their maturation to such wisdom more clear-cut (though not necessarily easier) than our culture tends to make our maturations today. In the New Mexico of the early years of the twentieth century, their small towns were steeped in Hispanic tradition, quite cut off from American culture at large. Both man and woman had distinct, clearly defined roles. Life was hard physically, and faith was severe: a strict moral code, a God waiting to cast wrongdoers into hell.

But somehow this severe outer frame served the soft, vulnerable essentials of self-surrender and love. By the time the couple had suffered their way into their mid-seventies, they had made peace with the land, with one another, with their God. One suspects that the core strength that brought them success was their willingness to keep picking themselves up, their refusal to let hard times or personal frustrations be the final word. There is no evidence that they ever had much money or educational opportunity. There is some evidence that at times they rubbed one another raw. But through good times and bad their commitment to one another—rooted in sexual attraction, disciplined by family responsibilities, strait-ened by religious convictions—kept turning the wheels of their cart until one day they crested a hill and came into the freedom to love and do what they would.

For those who no longer live in a well-defined culture, whose sexual roles and religious codes are anything but clear and strict, the possibility of growth may seem an entirely different proposition. With so many things up for grabs, is it reasonable to invest heavily in togetherness, give rough stones decades in which to rub one another smooth? Maybe only a few people feel they can answer yes with personal conviction, but this is because only a few people seem to ponder the realities of marriage seriously.

Essentially, the tasks of marriage are no different today than they were fifty years ago, nor is the essential fruition. People who succeeded then did the same things as people who succeed now, just as people who failed then (even if they stayed together) did the same things as people who fail now (whether they stay together or split apart). Marriage succeeds when people mature together. It fails when people do not mature together. The outer, social circumstances of any succeeding or failing are significant, because they have an important influence, but they are not the heart of the marital matter. The heart of the marital matter is ongoing work to mature together.

So the old, severe mores of the New Mexican couple did not guarantee their success, and the new, permissive mores of much contemporary American culture do not guarantee younger couples' failure. Marital success has always been somewhat detached from the prevailing mores, even at times opposed them, because the prevailing mores have always been prefabricated, somewhat ill-fitting. Thus wives stronger than their husbands have had to find ways to utilize their strength. Husbands more artistic than their wives have had to find ways to beautify their homes. In good marriages, love, honesty, and mutual respect have welded the couple together against ignorant outsiders. Happy spouses have been more creative than traditional mores would allow—more supple, playful, and sexy. Spouses can continue to be creative today. Whether the "traditional" mores be "anything goes" or "scripture says," spouses can continue to grow first-rate marriages.

The Mystery of God

If such first-rate marriages are to be Christian, they have to situate themselves in the mystery of God. For Jesus, that was the assumed treasure, the obvious pearl of great price. The mystery or kingdom or reign of his parental God gave Jesus his meat and drink, his love, healing, and compassion. When Jesus fled to the highest heavens, the mystery upheld his wings. When he descended to the deepest fathoms, the mystery guided his descent. The sparrows did not chirp without the knowledge of the

Father. The hairs of any child of the Father were numbered exactly. Because the Father so loved the world, the world had its being and savior. Because they did not know the Father, Jesus' enemies put him to death. The Spirit that led Jesus was the breath of the Father's love. The love of Jesus' disciples was the sign of the Father's power.

To be equal to such a description, the Christian God must be a mystery, a reality of an order different from the realities with which we normally deal. Normally we deal with things: delimited, definite entities. Things may cause us problems, leave us puzzles to solve, but they are not mysteries, fullnesses of implication too rich for us to handle. The only way that things or even people become mysteries is by suggesting the universal whole of which they are parts, the primordial be-ing in which they participate. The universal whole of reality, from distant galaxies to smallest nuclear particles, is mysterious, more than our minds can handle. The primordial be-ing (act of stepping forth from nothingness) that is the deepest interest of philosophy is mysterious, for we never create being in this absolute sense, always manipulate entities laid out before us.

Both the universal whole and the primordial dimension of being evoke "God," the ultimate, creative source. Both give any particular entity, stone or person, its framework, depth, and aura of holiness. In fact, God is the framework and depth of any thing, when we see it fully realistically. The overwhelming aspect of any thing, in religious perspective, is its grant of existence from God, the sheer wonder that it should happen to be. In the beginning God created the heavens and the earth, because they could not create themselves. They beg explanation from an other, independent, self-sufficient reality. But an independent, self-sufficient reality would be Reality, Being, something we'd have to capitalize. It would exist on a different level than any creature, as a cause and not an effect, a source and not a product. When deep thinkers such as Soren

Kierkegaard ponder matters such as these, they stammer forth difficult but useful formulas. According to Kierkegaard, there is an infinite qualitative distinction between the Creator and the creature. The One who causes others to be, who alone has sovereignty over existence, is utterly beyond our ken.

"All very well," the tolerant among you may be saying, "but what has this metaphysics to do with our interest in marriage?" Brutally put, it has everything to do with our interest in marriage, and we will trivialize marriage, as everything else in our lives, until we come to terms with it. The fact is, God is the physical foundation of all that we are and do. Augustine implied this when he famously said that God is more intimate to us than we are to ourselves. Paul gave it a christological turn when he more famously said, "He is before all things, and in him all things hold together" (Col. 1:17). Christ, the mysteriously "verbal" fullness of God, is before our marriages, and in him our marriages hold together. This is the faith-fact of the matter, the biblical bottom line. Until we settle our understanding of marriage on this bottom line, we diddle with superficialities, distract ourselves from the crux.

In our interpretation, the old couple leaning against their adobe house are poised precisely at the crux. Their life together has settled its foundation on the mystery of God, the source of the rain and fresh air, the sun and the birds. To be together in the face of, participant in, this mystery gives them a peace that surpasses the world's understanding. Their best response is keeping their tongues still, holding themselves in one place. It is what we call "contemplation": collected presence to God. When people can pray together contemplatively, be with God together, they have reached a high degree of marital maturity. For they know, in joint and marrow, that God is the bond between them, the love that makes them "one flesh." All the other sources and forms of their union flow out of this love and back into it. Conversation, work, sexual fusion, laughter, and tears are all flat without the mystery. They only round out to pregnant meaning and beauty when God's love comes to fertilize.

For those hungry to become one flesh, the gospel is stunningly consoling. The mysterious divine love that might work marital maturation has been poured forth in our hearts by the Holy Spirit. What eye has not seen, ear not heard—what has not entered the heart fully—God has made a down payment (*arrabon*) upon in the grace of Father-Son-Spirit. So the mystery of the Christian God does not make the prospects of marriage too hard to be borne but too good. Our highest hopes prove paltry and timid, compared to Jesus' God.

CHAPTER

2

The Life Cycle

Identity

IN DEALING WITH the old couple from New Mexico and our friends who are such natural parents, we have intimated themes of the life cycle. As psychologists of the past generation have discovered, both children and adults pass through discernible stages, and it can help considerably to understand them. For our purposes, the later stages of the life cycle, concerned with adulthood, are the most relevant. Of course, it is well for parents to know about the normal developmental stages of children, but that is somewhat peripheral to our main focus on the interaction of the marital partners. Therefore we only deal with identity, love, generativity, and wisdom—characteristics that Erik Erikson uses to describe the unfolding of ordinary adulthood.[1]

Identity is the crux of adolescence, what the turmoils are finally all about. Between childhood and adulthood, the person somewhat mature in body and catching up in personality struggles to grasp who he or she is going to be. Some of the data in this question are rudely objective: the child of Mr. and Mrs. So and So, the third sibling in the tapering row of five. Others are distressingly subjective: the ballerina with the unruly tutu, the shortstop with the iron hands. From biology to the trivia of last week's disasters, the young person canvasses the data. Perhaps most crucial, though, are appearance and competence. "I" am the string bean six feet two inches tall and weighing only 140 pounds. Or "I " am the peppy cheerleader who does the very best tumble. Or "I" am terrific on the computer, quite likely to find a good job in high tech. Or "I" so love little children that not even a terrible salary and lack of status will keep me from being a teacher.

All adults have vivid memories of the turmoils of adolescence, as well as the stubborn persistence of questions of identity long after their teens. It takes considerable experience, success, support from peers and lovers to fashion a solid, secure sense of self. When Freud made love and work the two central requisites of mental health, he summarized a lot of early crises. Until we know that we can relate warmly and honestly with others, giving and receiving affection, and that we can do something of social consequence, we feel shadowy and unformed, less than fully grown. This implies, of course, that marriage at the "normal" age of twenty-three or so will contribute to the process of "identification." Becoming the responsible, public lover of so and so, and then the parent of chips one, two, and three, adds weighty rings of identity, as does gaining a specialized degree or securing an estimable job. But in the ideal case, the work of identity has largely been accomplished before the two people marry. If even one is substantially unfinished, more adolescent than adult, the marriage begins with a serious handicap. When people say "I do," the "I" ought to be fairly well focused.

We shall deal more with the early stages of marriage in the next section where the topic is love, the force that binds two identities together. Here the specifically Christian dimension of identity begs consideration. What does it add to one's "I" to include in the canvass a strong faith in Jesus Christ? How do baptism, confirmation, and regular nurture at the Lord's Supper factor in? In theological perspective, they factor in as a patient process unfolding at the depths of the ordinary dynamics of the life cycle. The mysterious God revealed by Jesus abides in the center of the believer's personality, for comfort, challenge, and growth. The life of grace is not the opponent of ordinary maturation but its healer and uplifter. In traditional terms, "healing grace" (*gratia sanans*) counters the ravages of sin, while "elevating grace" (*gratia elevans*) takes the person up into the inner life of Father-Son-Spirit. Western Christianity has emphasized the former, Eastern Christianity the latter, but both aspects of grace are essential to a faithful understanding of human maturation. The life of Christ is not so much something we put on as something the Spirit broods, nurtures, and encourages in our depths.

At an opportune moment, therefore, young people who have worked at their faith may find the life of Christ personally significant. The "I" they utter probably will not reach Paul's mystical "It is no longer I who live, but Christ who lives in me; and the life I now live in the flesh I live by faith in the Son of God, who loved me and gave himself for me" (Gal. 2:20), but it can include a personal relation to Jesus, and a personal gratitude for God's love not just of humanity in general but of *me*, this specific sinner/saint. One has to be leery of young people's Christian confessions, especially when they occur in highly emotional contexts such as revivals or cursillios, but it makes sense that the Spirit might give a strong attachment to Jesus just when the personality is solidifying. Indeed, it would be a great gift to have one's first firm "I" implicitly identified with the beautiful Son of Man.

Love

For Erikson love is the force that joins two identities and keeps each from being stifled by self-concern. By contrast, people whose crystallization into personal identity is the limit of their growth strike us as both sad and boring. Fortunately we don't meet many people who have not at least tried to reach beyond themselves and love another adult. On occasion, however, we do run into someone who either hasn't tried very hard or has failed dismally, and the result is grimly instructive. Once, for example, we worked with a woman whose conversation and concern scarcely went beyond herself and her cats. She was bright, ambitious, successful, but so self-absorbed that, at first, it seemed an act; then, with a shiver, we realized it was not. The cats were an added misfortune, since they tempted us to paint her in their likeness. As they seemed concerned only with their own preening, so more often than not did she. As they seldom interested themselves in anyone else, so seldom did she. She was not dishonest or cruel, lazy or incompetent. She paid her bills and met her responsibilities. But something hellish was growing in the corners of her spirit, and it threatened to leave her utterly narcissistic.

The lovelessness of this woman did not immediately come across as a tragedy, so strong was her sense of self-possession. In another case, this time a young man, the tragedy was more apparent. Once again, there was no lack of talent or accomplishment. The surface was smooth, the smile bright. But signs of loneliness and sexual ambiguity grew more and more marked, and productivity started to falter. Now and then there were unexplained absences, as though drinking might be starting to be a problem. From time to time fantasy replaced objectivity as a way to handle hard problems. There was a supposed dimension of faith, but it seemed more a defense against hard looks at the self than an opening to the light of the Spirit. For lack of love, unwillingness or incapacity to open out and give, the man was digging a long future of bitterness.

Love is not a panacea, of course, and one doesn't turn it on at precise coordinates of the life-map. Rather, the sort of love we are considering is a natural outgrowth of a coalesced identity, the next step the healthy want to take. The development of the human personality is a twofold process of both greater differentiation and greater inclusion. Through the life cycle, we should become both more distinct and developed as specific personalities, and more sympathetic with, involved in, connected to the fates and fortunes of other people. So the love that brings young people solidly into adulthood both sharpens their personal identities and involves them intimately with another. This story is so frequent, so ordinary, that we can miss its wondrous strength.

Each spring, the new brides dotting the social pages remind us that another crop of young people are starting the marital adventure. Only the most stony-hearted among us do not wish them well and thank them for bucking up our own marital hopes. When we go to these June weddings, to add our bit of support and well-wishing, we usually return home a bit closer, maybe even holding hands. Year by year, the weightiness of the ceremony's implications seems to grow, while the ceremony itself lightens. The implications grow because we see that life is much richer, more complicated, more demanding, and more consoling than any couple can realize when they first decide to share it. The ceremony also lightens, because we realize that all the details that have caused so much fuss actually matter very little. The core act of the wedding ceremony is utterly simple and quite humorous, as in all good Christian comedy. What is impossible with human beings is possible with God, and the smiling community believes it.

"Love is blind," the wag says, "and marriage gives it vision." The wag means to be ironic, maybe even bitter, but the line runs away for a career of its own. Love is and is not blind. In first flush, it misses lots of aspects, makes light of serious problems, and tends to confuse hormones with grace. On the other hand, it sees deeper possibilities, more dazzling beauties, better reasons for joy than the loveless can even imagine. No one else knows, understands, sees the beloved as profoundly as the lover. That is the theme of ageless romance, Romeo and Juliet. True, it has parallels with mother love, father love, and even the love of good friends. But the love that marries two identities finally is the strongest and most perspicacious, the most flooded with biblical light. In biblical terms, Eve dazzles Adam because she is just what he needs, his soul's deep complement. When they know one another, through sexual exploration and suffusion, the dazzle becomes uniquely fruitful, a light that bears forth life.

Marriage gives such love vision, in the sense that it completes the picture. Only over time do the blinding first visions take on nuance, development, full revelation. Who the other is, the full range of the other's personality, only peeks out, and then marches forth, in peaceful living together. The kitchen and bathroom store up tales. The study and garden pitch in. The bedroom cedes to the nursery. The bills and in-laws have a say. What makes it fascinating rather than depressing, warming instead of too much, is a sense of outgrowth together, a growing confidence that one will not wake up a fat, self-satisfied cat.

Generativity

Somewhat identified, and then bonded in conjugal love, young adults settle down and try to become fruitful together. If the first years of marriage are apt to find them lost in the intrigue of one another, children and solid jobs usually shunt them into more public roles. The great passion of middle age (say thirty to sixty), in Erikson's view, is the desire to be productive. On the one side stand the forces of stagnation: selfishness, bad luck, incompetence, alienation of affection, irresponsibility. On the other side cluster the creativities that would make the person fruitful: parenthood, an imaginative approach to work, community service, religious maturation, deepening friendship with one's spouse. When the trade-off is favorable, the result is the strength or virtue of *care*. Generativity triumphs over stagnation because we care enough—for our children, our company, our town, our church, our spouse—to take all the guff and keep plugging. We have a need to be needed that is deeper than our need for leisure or self-indulgence. We know the good life is not a matter of martinis and racetracks but solid accomplishments.

A generative person is almost always content, frequently is quite happy. Homemakers, reliable employees, pillars of the church, and the like fill up their days with good deeds. If they are religiously mature they know that good deeds do not guarantee salvation, but they also know that vibrant faith expresses itself in good deeds, acts of love of God and love of neighbor. People who are not generative don't care for the next generation or the neighborhood. They tend to chew on their own innards and then wonder why they taste so much bile.

All too often we have seen this professionally. Again and again, people who do not produce creatively at work grow bitter and negative. Step by step they erect an increasingly paranoid psychic structure to blame others for their own shortcomings. It is because their work is so thorough, or of such high quality, or they themselves are of such perfectionist temper that they have gone unapplauded. It is because bosses have favored those who fawned, or they themselves were courageously outspoken, or the powers above came from another ethnic group (or school or church or geographic region). Poor people. If only they would face themselves in the mirror, broaden their horizons, and find other ways to make a contribution. If only they would let God be the judge, unclench their fists and let go.

True, there are neurotics among the productive, paranoids among the artistic. But the fully generational, those whose creativity and warmth give life to another round of offspring, use their productivity as a springboard to generosity. Once blessed with a little success, they give over their competitiveness, rejoice when others come into the limelight. When they gain positions of responsibility, they make them occasions for nurturing younger people's careers, fostering subordinates' creativities. Indeed, the best administrators we've seen quite consciously conceive of their work as enabling a team to pull together and accomplish more than the isolated individuals could alone. Like the best parents, the best administrators are proudest when their protégés win big or even little victories.

Care, generativity, nurturing—the key drive of middle

age utilizes several different modes and names. In the home it is parenting: raising those one has brought into being. In the classroom it is educating: leading out the potentialities of fresh young minds. In the church it is ministry: providing succor, insight, supports of faith. In the medical profession it is service: putting oneself out to bind up wounds, restore confidence. And so it goes, from profession to profession, role to role. In business, town politics, and community projects millions of adults keep society functioning, ensure that opportunity and culture will be handed on. Some, to be sure, seek mainly their own power and glory. Their care is not so much service as self-promotion. But they are neither the people most crucial to human progress, nor the people in whom the fruits of the Spirit are most manifest.

The people in whom the fruits of the Spirit are most manifest tend to be humble folk: moms and dads, grannies and uncles, teachers and healers who day by day secure the bread and uncork the wine. Huub Oosterhuis, a Dutch poet, has a nice prayer for these and similar good Samaritans:

> Let us pray
> for all those who have dedicated themselves
> to the service of their neighbors,
> for those who are engaged in social work,
> for all members of charitable organizations,
> for all who nurse the sick and aged.

> Let us pray
> that they do not do their work of love
> only to be seen . . .
> and that they resist the temptation
> to exert power over other people
> but that, in all simplicity,
> they give themselves to others as Jesus did
> . . . .

> Let us pray
> for all ministers and priests
> and for all who hold some office in their church,

that they may imitate the High Priest Jesus
who did not think his dignity a thing to be grasped.

And let us pray for all churches
that they may continue,
in poverty and without pretentions,
the work of service to all . . .
that Jesus came to do.
We pray that they may avoid compulsion
and offer no false security,
but present the gospel to [all people]
and inspire faith.[2]

Wisdom

We have been playing themes of the life cycle under the
assumption that a rough knowledge of how adults tend to
grow should help couples better understand the dynamics
of their marriage. If change is the law of life, and married
couples are trying to share life intimately, knowing the
"ordinary" patterns of change that the maturing human
personality goes through ought to be a marital plus. So,
we have traced the progress from the consolidation of an
identity that marks the beginning of adulthood proper,
through the bonding of two identities in love, to the
expansion of love in generativity—care for children, work,
social institutions, and other fruits or connections to which
marital love leads. As anyone who reflects in the slightest
will see, identity, love, and generativity do not stand to
one another as discrete stages or separate preoccupations.
The human personality does not unfold, grow, or mature
in a strictly linear fashion. A much better figure is an
ascending spiral or helix: a corkscrew that keeps taking old
edges or themes up into new realms of (psychic) space.
Thus identity, love, and generativity all have stages or
forms prior to their dominance of a particular life cycle
period and stages or forms after it. All have seeds from
way back in childhood and later fruits in old age. The
same pattern holds for the last adult virtue or preoccupation that we consider, the wisdom that comes to center

stage in old age. It, too, has anticipatory forms before sixty, and we may believe that it continues to deepen in heaven.

For Erikson this wisdom is the ability, the strength, to love life in the face of death. It is the power to confront all the dissolutions of the self and imperfections of the world and still emerge integral, whole, a finished product. Of course, the "finish" of wisdom is not like that of a carving or a car. Older people don't one day suddenly say, "I'm done," and hop onto the table to be mummified. Rather the wise or fully mature slowly come to a peaceful acceptance of their mortality, limitation, and undeniable accomplishments. Whatever time they have left they will treasure, but they begin to put behind them the driving, striving, almost compulsively generational energies of middle age and give themselves over to the rhythms and flow of the cosmos. Thus from time to time they speak in tones reminiscent of Confucius, the sage who has given billions of Chinese their highest model of completion: "By the time I was seventy I could do what I wished, for my wishes and the Way were one. If I hear the Way in the morning, in the evening I can die content." The "Way" (*Tao*) of which Confucius speaks is the objective pattern of things, what the West might call the will of God.

When death, our completion in this earthly form, begins to become personally real, something we can hear murmuring in our own blood, the personality naturally turns reflective. The psychologist C. G. Jung therefore divided his patients into those dealing with the problems typical of the first half of life and those struggling with the problems of the second half of life (when they had begun to grapple with their own mortality). In no case, he said, had he met a patient in the second half of life whose essential problems weren't religious. By the very nature of the case, the preview of our coming death makes us start to take stock, get our inner houses in order, reconcile ourselves to what we have actually become. Whereas in the first half of life we are more potential than actual, have arrayed before us a groaning table of selves we still might become, in the second half of life we have to live with the limiting effects of our actual choices, relegate the roads not taken, the selves not developed, to the realm of interesting but secondary regrets.

We authors, for example, have to date developed into teacher and writer. At our ages (middle, but facing less time ahead than behind), the likelihood of radically different options in work, marriage, or personality structures is steadily diminishing, since it grows harder and harder to make the case that more would be gained by such change than lost. This does not mean no openness at all to other options, straight plunging down to stick in the mud. It just means being realistic about the momentum built up in our present directions, and being willing to hear the slowly growing voices within that ask us to take stock of who we are more and more definitively becoming.

These voices, we believe, are a gentle summons to wisdom. They have not yet penetrated our marrow, begun to be our souls' master-song, but they are making us more reflective, ironic, detached from all those roads not taken. (The main value in musing about roads not taken—why we did not become psychologists, politicians, or bishops— lies in staying in touch with the intuitive, interpersonal, and leadership qualities we showed as talented teenagers. As it is profitable now and then to return home, revisit in memory the scenes of childhood when mother and father stamped one's tender psyche, so it is profitable occasional- ly to imagine how talents that have become secondary might have developed had we made them primary, be- cause it helps us retain a bit of such talents' strength.) As one slips out of the middle stages, to approach retirement and consummation, the possible has to cede to the actual, to what one *de facto* has done with the Master's talents. And then even the talents have to fall away, as one realizes that only the Master should dominate. Others plant, we water, but only God gives the increase death asks, our wholehearted yes to God's will.

Male-Female Complementarity

Identity, love, generativity, and wisdom are virtues that all adults require. Male or female, we need to gain a distinct "I," connect intimately with one or more other "I's," make our love fruitful, and reach a view of the whole sufficient that we can love life in the face of death. Still, marriage usually comes about because two people approach these and other aspects of being human in intriguingly different ways. To be human in a male body and psyche is sufficiently different from being human in a female body and psyche to give man and woman an inexhaustible play, fertility, and complementarity. The French phrase "Vive la différence!" captures the energizing quality of the distinctions between women and men. The sparks that carry across those distinctions not only lead to the birth of the next generation, they also almost force us to be fascinated with very concrete forms of the most basic question life puts to us: "What does it mean to be human?" As Genesis suggests, it means to be male-female, woman-man, the new third thing that emerges from the marriage of sex a to sex b. As Plato's myth in the *Symposium* agrees, the most adequate picture of "humanity" would be something round, four-legged and four-armed, with all the qualities of both sexes. Our erotic desire to unite sexually is powered by a sense that we ought to experience being human as such a roundness or wholeness.

At any rate, it seems useful to consider the main differences that psychologists of the life cycle currently find men and women to exhibit, in order the better to understand what the Christian marital ideal of becoming "one flesh" is likely to entail. Simplistically put, males tend to strive for differentiation, females for integration, and the mature individual personality (to say nothing of the mature marriage) clearly demands both. By differentiation we mean the distinguishing of oneself as an individual, separation from the group, development of independence and autonomy, and strong sense of self-reliance that characterize (or stereotype) the mature male in our culture. By integration we mean the sense of being part of a larger whole, uniting to something more than oneself, participating in a process, destiny, and reality that is richer and more enhancing than one's solitary ego—characteristics that dominate the strivings of the mature female in our culture. To date, the researchers who have been most influential in plotting adult intellectual and moral development have tended to stress differentiation. As more women have entered the research ranks, and feminist consciousness has made a bigger impact, integration has begun to come in for a fuller appreciation.[3] The likelihood for the next round of researches is that the questionnaires and interviews will reflect and seek a better balance. The current feeling, summarily, is that the fully matured personality, male or female, should exhibit both differentiation and integration, be at the same time a distinct, independent individual and a willing player in larger dramas, works, or entities.

We may leave the technical aspects of such research and reflection to the professional psychologists, since our interest here is simply the illumination of Christian marriage. For that interest, the stimulating suggestion seems to be that men of the currently middle-aged generation probably have received role models that stressed independence and self-reliance, while their female counterparts have received models that stressed locating the self in the midst of a larger group (family, work group, circle of friends, church). This is not to say that men never heard about teamwork, women could never be solitary or have what Virginia Woolf called a room of their own. It is just to suggest that overall, in terms of general tendencies, men recently have been brought up to keep pushing for advancements, growths, higher accomplishments that would make them stand out in bolder individuality, while women recently have been brought up to grease the gears, draw others out, find satisfaction as part of a flourishing group (the family especially, but other groups as well). When adults have intuitively understood these tendencies and relativized them by a sense of proportion and humor, the sexes have managed fairly well. (After all, there have been some fine marriages.) When adults have not understood these tendencies well or handled them lightly, the tendencies have produced a lot of emotional retardation and suppressed fury. The hard-charging male who is handicapped in the area of feelings and the sweet female who is manipulative to the core are but the grosser miscarriages.[4]

We see these differences somewhat less judgmentally when we compare the ways that men's and women's groups tend to do business. The men tend to set things up confrontationally and stress the supposed reasons pro and con. The women tend to build on one another's contributions and seldom reject any suggestion completely. In the women's proceedings, sensitivity to the feelings of all group members is more prominent. In the men's proceedings objective analysis of the given problem is more prominent. Both instinctive methods have their assets and liabilities. The men can be sharper in analysis and more willing to say no or handle bad news. The women can be more successful in eliciting a broad base of support, rooted in most participants' feeling that they are important parts of the whole. The men run the danger of not knowing or being honest about their real feelings and so making "rationality" a wrong-headed dodge. The women run the danger of circling endlessly and being unwilling to come to the crunch. The women's keener social intelligence makes them instinctively the better politicians. The men's greater freedom from what others think tends to make them the tougher enemies of some forms of evil. And— more interesting than any of these quite debatable generalizations—the interactions of men and women in mixed groups make for dynamics that are almost more fascinating than the business the group is supposed to be getting done. Surely in a wise consummation of the marital life-cycle, a couple will have laughed and brooded over these dynamics a great deal.

3

A Theology of Christian Marriage

A Covenantal Framework

WE TURN NOW to some theological reflections, asking the tradition of faith to help us illumine the graced dimension of the marital life cycle. These reflections are not in competition with the psychological or common-sensical observations we have made thus far. If we believe that grace heals and uplifts human nature, we have to think that everything that genuinely repairs or advances the human personality is pleasing in the sight of God. As the Greek church father Irenaeus said, "God's glory is human beings fully alive." The mystery revealed by Jesus to be a parental love does not want our craven infancy but our robust maturity. It gives God no satisfaction to see people wander into sickness, stagnation, neurosis, or frustration. We have minds in order to ponder, wills in order to take our lives in hand. That is the implication of the parable of the talents (Matt. 25:14–30). God doesn't associate us with the sloths or the slugs. We're supposed to be bright-eyed and bushy-tailed.

Putting our bright little eyes to the biblical symbolism, let us first consider the figure of the covenant. Under Moses, we are told, Israel struck a covenant or compact with God. By the time of Jeremiah, Yahweh would be their God, and they would be his people (Jer. 7:23). The basic metaphor in the background of this biblical figure is the treaty between king and vassal that was commonplace in the ancient Near East. The king would promise to protect the vassal. The vassal would promise to work (or fight, or otherwise serve) the king. It was a business deal, a *quid pro quo*. Eventually the biblical theologians rose above this commercial or low-level political analogy, but there always remained a sense of mutual rights and duties.

Indeed, it was reflection on the rupture of the covenantal balance of rights and duties that led prophets such as Hosea to interiorize the covenant. What remained of the business deal, or the personal relationship, when Israel reneged on its duties, went into moral default? From his own painful marital experience, Hosea drew forth an intimate analogy. Pondering the infidelities of his wife Gomer, he realized that the best part of him could not abandon his love for her. Despite his anger, shame, sense of injustice, intuitions of responsibility and guilt, she still moved him to the core, he still wanted her with him. In a stunning moment of insight, he realized that God just might feel the same way about Israel. Despite all Israel's wantonness—lack of faith, defection to pagan nature gods, failure to enact social justice—God might still bear Israel an affection, a love, that went deeper than his disgust, anger, or heart-sickness.

These were symbolic ways of thinking, Hosea knew, but what else have human beings ever had? It has always been our fate to ponder the ultimate mystery with fragile analogies from human experience. The more profound the experience or poetic the symbolization the better the pondering, but no pondering has ever reached a God's eye view of things. For Hosea the most searing, maturing, educational experiences of his life had been forced upon him by Gomer. He felt called by God to put these experiences to use, and the result was a recasting of the covenant: God and Israel related not as king and vassal but as husband and wife. Through prayer and reflection, Hosea discovered that nothing Israel did (or failed to do) could break the covenant. God's love for Israel, like Hosea's own love for Gomer, was somehow unconditional. Without calling wrong right, or retracting the demand that fidelity be rendered, or denying the pain that infidelity had caused, the Divine Spouse would go on loving the human partner because of the Spouse's own goodness and nature as pure and recreative love.

Now the point for our purposes is not so much the particulars of the relation between God and human beings as the prophet's spontaneous casting of human intimacy in the framework of God's dealing with human beings. If the initial movement seems to be from Hosea's marriage to God's relation with Israel, further reflection shows that the later movement is from God's intimacy with Israel back to Hosea's marriage. Indeed, it could not be otherwise. Having mounted up to God by way of human analogy and had some light shone on the likely ways that God operates, we return to human affairs chastened, refurbished, with eyes cleansed. If Hosea began by getting a new insight into the covenant, he concluded with a new insight into marriage.

God must be more than a grudging partner to a legal contract if the poetry and redemption of the Old Testament are to make sense. God must be an unconditional lover if the teaching and career of Jesus are to ring true. The covenant of Israel with God becomes the New Testament figures of body of Christ and union of branches with vine. The prophet's marital symbolism is taken up by Ephesians and Revelation to illumine the union of Christ with his people. For faith, therefore, marriage has a richly covenantal framework. What two people do in wedding and making a common life takes its best significance, its most helpful orientation, from the patient, forgiving, utterly intimate dealings of God with human beings.

Where a legal contract remains outside the two parties, however much they may strive to take it to mind and heart, a marital contract flows between the two people, as they make love and bear many kinds of increase. In this flow, the covenantal fidelity of God can stand as a most consoling and helpful model. Neither death nor life, angels nor principalities, things past nor things to come can separate us from the love of God. By the help of God, neither weakness nor poverty nor stupidity nor even sin need separate us from the partner who is flesh of our flesh. The constancy of God, who makes the rain fall and sun shine whether we are saints or sinners, should be less an embarrassment than an encouragement. The more we rely on *that* source of strength, the more likely we are to be constant ourselves.

The Symbolism of the Church

From the Hebrew Bible, the theology of the covenant invites spouses to consider themselves bonded the way that Yahweh was bonded to Israel. From the New Testament, the theology of the church invites spouses to consider themselves integrated into one common reality. In the Pauline writings, the followers of Christ make with him one body, a common organic life. Reflecting on this, the early church fathers sometimes spoke of "The Whole Christ," meaning the unity of head and members. This mystical entity was suggested by such scriptural passages as Acts 9:1–5, where Saul, the persecutor of Christians, is converted to the realization that one who persecutes the church persecutes Jesus himself:

> Saul, still breathing threats and murder against the disciples of the Lord, went to the high priest and asked him for letters to the synagogues at Damascus, so that if he found any belonging to the Way, men or women, he might bring them bound to Jerusalem. Now as he journeyed he approached Damascus, and suddenly a light from heaven flashed about him. And he fell to the ground and heard a voice saying to him, "Saul, Saul, why do you persecute me?" And he said, "Who are you, Lord?" And he said, "I am Jesus, whom you are persecuting."

The identification that Jesus makes with his disciples is such that their fate becomes his own. Through what theologians sometimes call an "extension" of the Incarnation, the Word of God that took flesh in Jesus of Nazareth continues to be present—visible, audible, tangible—in Jesus' "members." That is why the unity of those members is so important, as John 17:20–21 makes plain. There Jesus follows his prayer for his present disciples with a prayer for the generations that will succeed them: "I do not pray for these only, but also for those who believe in me through their word, that they may all be one; even as thou, Father, art in me, and I in thee, that they also may be in us, so that the world may believe that thou has sent me." The unity of Jesus' members is to be the prime sign to the world that Jesus' mission is true, Jesus' Father is credible. And the unity to which those members may aspire is the very highest unity there is, the perfect identification of Father and Son (and Spirit). The divine has so identified itself with the human that everything human is potentially sacramental or iconic. What the Father did in sending the Son makes things of space and time, blood and bone, presences of the holy ultimacy on which creation itself depends.

Once again, our point is not to develop the particulars of ecclesiology, as in the prior section it was not to develop the particulars of covenantal theology. The point for our purposes is to set Christian marriage in the deepest possible perspective. This would appear to be the way that God has chosen to identify with us human beings. The nuptial and bridal symbolism associated with the church, and the central notion that the church is the body of Christ, encourage us to think of marriage as capable of producing a much more complete communion of the two spouses than otherwise we might imagine. Historically, many cultures have not expected a great deal from marriage. By and large, procreation has overshadowed the possibilities for the two spouses themselves. Without at all neglecting procreation, or failing to appreciate how deeply parenthood and espousal are bound to intertwine, we want to use the revelations of the Christian God's overtures of intimacy to remove any undue restriction on marriage's potential. We want to say to prior or extra-Christian histories that they have seen only a portion of what the union of woman and man might bring about.

To be sure, Christian theology always runs the danger of hyperbole, getting carried away by the mind-boggling claims that scripture makes for God's love. As the Incarnation actually proceeded day by day, with Jesus having to eat, drink, sleep, and put up with drones, so our marriages are composed of very ordinary, and demanding, little increments. But through the ordinary, even humdrum, particulars of his days, Jesus revealed the utter goodness of God, and through our humdrum particulars the spirit of Jesus is continuing the revelation, salvation, and redemption of Jesus. In sociological terms, Jesus sought, and in principle achieved, a complete identification with his followers (who in turn stand for all humankind). The retrospective theologies of Paul and John make this clear: Jesus sought and achieved a union with his people closer than that of bride and groom, vine and branches. His cause and life were theirs, and vice versa. So for Paul to live was Christ and to die was gain. For John, Christian life meant abiding in Christ's spirit, an insertion through Christ into the inner trinitarian love-life of the divinity itself. Eastern Christian theology summarized these sociological splendors by speaking of "divinization" (*theosis*): we are taken up into the very life and nature of God; the realest thing about us is the life of God in us.

Set Christian marriage in such an audacious framework and what possibilities for intimacy between the spouses can you deny out of hand? The two who marry are candidates for divinization, and their marriage is the context, the vehicle, the vocation through which God plans to take their lives over. The "take-over," of course, is gentle and noncompulsive, not the enemy of the spouses' individual or conjoint freedom but that freedom's perfecting. Together, in a union of mind, body, soul, heart, and affection, wife and husband try to open themselves to the love-life of God that knocks at their door. Now gracefully and now with the staggers, they pray, remember, sin, forget, fall, pick themselves up—in the framework of God's romancing of them, the prodigal Father's going out to welcome back the prodigal son. The church tells spouses that no ideal of communion need seem too ambitious for them, because God's achievement of communion with human beings has opened every possibility.

The Criteria of Growth

When we ask about the actual forms that growth in divine life as a married couple might take, we shift from speculative to practical theology. Where speculative theology tries to reason out some of the implications of the splendid symbols of scripture, practical theology seeks to realize those symbols' fruits, help people learn how to make divinization flower in their own hearts and homes. Among the most useful subspecies of such practical theology is what sometimes goes by the name of "the discernment of spirits." Drawing upon passages of scripture that describe what the new life of Christ ought to look like, and upon the trials and errors through which saints and sinners have hammered out the regularities of the spiritual life, the discernment of spirits would lay before us some of the touchstones of authentic progress.[1] In this section we try to apply them to the case at hand, the development of Christian spouses.

In chapter 5 of Galatians Paul has written one of the classical scriptural texts on the discernment of spirits, contrasting the "works of the flesh" with the "fruit of the Spirit":

> Now the works of the flesh are plain: fornication, impurity, licentiousness, idolatry, sorcery, enmity, strife, jealousy, anger, selfishness, dissension, party spirit, envy, drunkenness, carousing, and the like. I warn you, as I warned you before, that those who do such things shall not inherit the kingdom of God. But the fruit of the Spirit is love, joy,

peace, patience, kindness, goodness, faithfulness, gentleness,
self-control; against such there is no law.

—Galatians 5:19–23

This is a quite basic, commonsensical discrimination of
the things that manifest an ungodly temper from the
things that manifest the upbuilding Spirit. The works of
the flesh show a personality that takes little account of
either the divine life granted to it or the call of the holy
mystery to embark upon such a life. To be embedded in
"flesh" to such a degree is to have closed oneself to the
knock of God upon one's door, the drawing of the Spirit
toward light and love. By contrast, the Spirit manifests
itself in love, joy, peace, and the rest. The person centered in God, open to the holy mystery, surrendered to
her Creator is being knit into wholeness, cleansed to a
purer and purer loveliness. Later purifications of the
Spirit may occur in the stages prior to special holiness
when the saints go through patches of discouragement,
dryness, and severe testing. At this ground-level of Paul's
discussion, however, the distinction between those on the
right track and those being led astray is quite clear.

The signs do not change very much, at this level, when
we ask about their application to Christian marriage. At a
general, overall glance, one can tell the basically healthy
marriage from the basically disordered, the union that is
prospering from the union that is in deep spiritual trouble.
In Christian perspective, one cannot have a growing,
prospering marriage unless both partners agree that the
spirit of God, the outreach of their faith, is their prime
treasure. By pursuing that pearl of great price, they find
themselves expanding in love, joy, peace, patience, and
the rest. (It does not work so well the other way, using
God to make one happy. Only when we pursue God with
as few strings attached as possible do genuinely religious
love, joy, peace, and the rest begin to flower.) The family
that get drunk, commit fraud, or slander their neighbors
together may stick to one another like thieves or co-

conspirators, but they will not experience a deep peace, be surprised by an otherworldly joy.

At a level somewhat more advanced, when the couple have been slugging along for a decade or two, the signs become slightly more subtle. Gross temptations to infidelity, violence, or envy may still arise from time to time, but the more prevailing concerns are apt to be various expressions of discouragement. We grow too soon old and too late smart. The skip can go from our step, we can feel stuck deep in a rut. It is characteristic of the Paraclete, the Holy Spirit as advocate, to help us counter these bouts of discouragement. It is characteristic of the enemies of our advancement (which we can collectively symbolize as Satan) to deepen our discouragement. The good Spirit makes a gentle entrance, especially at times of quiet and prayer, to help us restore perspective, purify motivation. Then we are apt to realize that what is getting us down is less our lack of progress in faith than such questionable "evils" as our expanding waistline, or our receding hairline, or our failure to move up the salary ladder. These, the Spirit reminds us, are things after which the heathen rush. For them to trouble a couple gifted with the riches of divine life is rather incongruous, something to blush and laugh about.

The whispers of the evil one are those that tell us it is hopeless, too much for us, not worth our continuing to try. Where all God asks is our best this day, the satanic whispers stretch out before us years and years of continual struggle. Where God has constantly promised to forgive our sins, the satanic whispers try to maneuver us into corners of guilt, make us feel we have no right to show up for prayer or start a heart to heart session with our spouse or open our sorried spirits to God or a spiritual director. The main criteria of progress, then, are decreasing self-concern, increasing faith in God's power to untie our tangles, deepening understanding of the wonders hidden in the simple sentence, "Even when our hearts condemn us, God is greater than our hearts" (1 John 3:20, AP).

Good Times and Bad

The theological assumption behind such discernmental criteria as moving toward John the Baptist's "He must increase, I must decrease" is the active help of the Holy Spirit. If we are to contend with the real, mysterious God, we must let many this-worldly securities go, learn to walk step by step in faith. If we are to become one flesh, grow a marriage worthy of the possibilities faith holds out, we must depend on the One whom Christ has left as our Paraclete. The hallmark of our essential dependence on the Spirit, our adequate if hardly heroic faith, will be a fundamental peace and joy. Below all our real financial worries, physical pains, distresses about the kids, anxieties about the church or the nation, the Spirit offers us a core peace. At times we may doubt the reality of this peace, so bruised and lacerated may our minds and hearts feel. At times it may break out so vividly that we think we have flown to the highest heaven. But most days it will play as a quiet *cantus firmus*, relativizing both good times and bad. Only our radical rejection of God, our deeply willful no to the creative mystery, will take it entirely away.

The traditional spiritual wisdom about oscillations in moods, days when we are up and days when we are down, is that we should remember they are temporary. When we are up, on top of the world, we should give ourselves a bit of anchoring by remembering how down we were last week. We should not do this to be killjoys but to prevent unrealistic expectations, foolish overcommitments, and the pride that forgets how frail we are without the Spirit's lift. When we are down, carrying the weight of the world, we should move in the opposite direction, recalling that last week things looked rosy, previous depressions passed, and that now is a time to learn (almost humorously) how little we have to brag or posture about.

With time, this kind of advice or instinctive good sense makes the stable, dependable sort of personality for whom most of us are so grateful. At work, at home, in our

church circle, do we not find ourselves especially grateful
for the boss or grandmother or secretary who has such an
even keel, who so constantly keeps the fair side out? Only
when we have matured a bit do we realize how few people
manage such cheer effortlessly. In most cases, persistent
peace and joy are solid gifts of the Spirit enhanced by not
a little religious generosity on the part of the recipient.
The fact that a relatively large number of people do come
to this maturity is one of the most hopeful social signs. It
suggests that the God who is not without witness anywhere
frequently is present in humble smiles, almost impercepti-
ble bits of grit.

The application of these ascetical generalizations to
marriage is almost too easy. Would not many spouses,
were they to make explicit their prayers of thanksgiving,
place the day-by-day cheerfulness of their partner high
atop the list? Like rain falling on a tin roof is the chatter of
a nagging spouse. Like vertigo and an upset stomach is
the effect of a mercurial, now hot now icy spouse. Saints
preserve us from the household in which one must wet a
finger and test the air each morning. God help the kids
and partner of a person who holds greedily to hurts, will
not forgive and forget. On a day-by-day basis, a peaceful,
loving, dependable personality is one of the greatest gifts
we can offer. If so, it is one of the main gifts for which we
ought to pray.

Christians marry for better or worse, richer or poorer,
sickness or health, agreeing to go forward together, however
God wishes to be with them. They marry for good times
and bad. And the grace of their marriage is that if they
share to any depth at all the good times are doubled and
the bad times halved. Indeed, what are "good times" if
not the occasions when we overflow with joy and feel the
biblical measure for sharing it? What are "bad times" if
not the pains, guilts, depressions that make us uncom-
municative, drive us out of communion? When the biblical writer said that it is not good for human beings to be
alone (Gen. 2:18), it was not the solitude of peace and

quiet that was vetoed. It was the isolation, alienation, or sense of disconnection that take away life's shine and make it inconceivable that the morning stars ever sang together or the angels of God ever shouted for joy.

Jollying one another, listening, offering perspective, wrapping arms around, spouses join forces against the dark nights of depression, frequently turning them into quiet purifications. When they are shrewd, they do not focus on the other's troubled emotions so much as on the other's troubled self. They know that there is a time for grieving, repenting, tasting the dust and ashes of creaturehood or mortality. They know that spiritual growth can demand frightening sacrifice, the leaving behind of what seem essential parts of the self. But those who comfort wisely trust the processes of the Spirit, and the integrity of their spouse, to make profit of the currently trying experience. Their vow is to be nearby, empathetic and attuned, in good times and bad. No matter how shabby their fidelity to this vow, how many times they fail to meet its high standard, they do not repudiate its substance, for their love has bound them to the other like the love of the classical Greek friendship: Their spouse is the other half of their own soul.

One Flesh

Once we used one of our books as a required reading in a course.[2] A student in the throes of a painful divorce said it made her very angry, because it seemed to paint an impossible ideal. She was struggling, down in the dumps, and the high flights of the book only made her feel more depressed. It was a sobering reaction to hear, and we tucked it away for future reference. While the woman was balanced and honest enough to admit that her own raw emotions probably had made her hypersensitive, we felt bad for having increased her pain. The good news ought to comfort the afflicted, not rub salt in their wounds. The ideals we propose ought to seem attractive and alluring, not impossible of achievement. Of course making God the central reference, rather than ourselves, immediately improves the situation. But it cannot be overemphasized that God holds out the wonders of grace, the far reaches of divine life and marital maturity, *even to us,* these very ordinary, quite begrimed dullards and sinners. As in Jesus' time, it is the blind God offers the chance to see, the lepers God would cleanse, the poor who have the good news preached to them.

When we talk about becoming one flesh, therefore, we are talking about a process that can begin right where any married couple, no matter how blind or poor, currently find themselves. The ideal admits of various degrees of realization, and some couples will have to struggle harder than others, but both *a priori* and *a posteriori* considerations convince us that all Christian marriages have a strong impetus toward a union, a new whole, that merges the partners in something beyond their private selves. This is not just rhetorical but as real as the sunrise, the rain, the gap in a seven-year-old's teeth. By *a priori* considerations we mean the things one can expect from the outset, in the nature of the case, because one can infer them from the very structure of marital grace. By *a posteriori* considerations we mean concrete evidences, things one finds actually occurring among specific marital partners.

From the outset one can expect that talk about becoming one flesh is not just pie in the sky, because the Bible does not babble irresponsibly. One of the Bible's most persuasive characteristics is its sober realism about human nature, its assurance to us that Jesus knows what transpires in the human heart. For the Song of Songs, a book of secular love poetry, to be taken into the Hebrew canon was a solid vote for God's realism about human emotion, a solid endorsement of the analogy between erotic love on the human level and God's romancing of the human heart. Later such Christian mystics as Bernard of Clairvaux seconded the endorsement, seeing the Song of Songs as an allegory of the soul's dalliances with God.

The "flesh" being discussed in Christian scripture is the whole human being, emotion, reason, and musculature. The oneness being touted as the marital ideal, and as the image of God's communion with us in grace, is the overlap and increasing commonality of cause that one finds in household after household, bedroom after bedroom. Sometimes a marriage seems to move two steps forward and one step back. Sometimes it has patches of friction, misconnection, running in neutral. People can join in body and separate in mind. They can be apart physically yet think the same thoughts. The variations, ups, downs, and side ways are too numerous to count. There is only one constant: Every marriage has becoming one flesh as its natural, inbuilt goal.

Consider, for example, the simple biology of marriage (although no human biology is really simple, not connected to psychology, sociology, and theology). People marry for the sake of physical union. If they want just mental union, congeniality of mind, they can remain fast friends. Marriage implies the full mutuality or reciprocal suffusion symbolized in sexual intercourse. Fitted together sexually, the partners are one flesh literally. And from this literal integration come children, a new sort of single flesh. The pink flesh of Baby Jones is an individual, a unified whole, that represents the union of Mother and Father Jones. From the x's and y's of the chromosomes to the coordinating of Father's chin and Mother's eyes, Baby Jones takes from each of his or her sources, making the parents' confluence permanent, ongoing, something they have formed from their own substance and set forth on an independent career in the outside world.

None of this is news, anything all of us haven't seen, thought, flirted with dozens of times. On the other hand, none of it is commonplace, understandable, or unchallenging. For all their billions, babies each and all enflesh a miracle. The more we learn about the details of conception, gestation, birth, and early childhood, the more astounded we become. What the pediatricians call "nature" is a program of unimaginable sophistication. Not only do genetic triggers direct the growth of little fingernails and frontal lobes, but they also prime the baby to seduce his or her parents, elicit care, and beguile delighted onlookers into giving it the attention and stimulus it needs. Like the other aspects of the ideal of one flesh that we shall consider, the simple facts of intercourse and birth bespeak an amazing accomplishment. Whether given partners feel they should take much credit for it or not, their minimal levels of union and fruitfulness already provide material for hundreds of grateful meditations.

CHAPTER
4

Romance

Eros

WE BEGIN THE movement toward one flesh when a spark
of interest and then desire for union touches the tinder of
our need for love. The Greeks called this desirous love
"eros," and they did not mean at all the crude incitement
of lust that the "erotic" movies advertised in the newspa-
pers now promise. The Greeks meant the flow of energy,
mental and emotional both, that occurs when one is
dazzled by something beautiful and wants to learn more
about it, join oneself more fully to it. Socrates went so far
as to say that eros was the only talent or competence he
would claim. He knew that when this god swept away his
spirit he was at a high point of his life.

Many lives are blessed with high points of erotic love,
times when experience peaks in a wonder that makes the
heart stop, a sense of yearning that suddenly reveals what
human being, male-femaleness, is for. Testimonies sprout
all over, even in such an unlikely place as a mystery novel
about transporting horses and political subversives:

> You couldn't say it was reasonable, it was just electric. I
> found out between one heartbeat and the next what all the
> poets throughout the ages had been going on about. I
> understood at last why Roman Antony threw away his
> honor for Egyptian Cleopatra, why Trojan Paris caused a
> ten years' war abducting Greek Helen, why Leander drowned
> on one of his risky nightly swims across the Dardanelles to
> see Hero. The distance from home, the mystery, the
> unknownness, were a part of it; one couldn't feel like that
> for the girl next door. But that didn't explain why it hadn't

happened before; why it should be this girl, this one alone who fizzed in my blood.

I stood on the cool stone airport floor and felt as if I'd been struck by lightning; the world had tilted, the air was crackling, the gray February day blazed with light, and all because of a perfectly ordinary girl who sold souvenirs to tourists.[1]

The protagonist of the novel is fortunate enough to have the girl reciprocate his eros, so they share a new sense of the glory of the stars, the changes that come when one is suddenly living at 125 percent capacity. Only the reader most impatient to get back to the criminal gore does not enjoy this interlude, find it a well-wrought reminder of what it is that keeps the race going. This is the reason a biblical man might work seven years, and then another seven, and count his abuse light compared to the bride he'd won (Gen. 20–30). This is the reason the bard might compare his lover to a summer's day and find the lover winning handily, the reason Elvira Madigan could become an indelible visualization of Mozart's Piano Concerto no. 21. The Song of Songs claims that love of this type is strong as death. Common testimony broadens the claim, reporting that when eros is carrying us we feel immortal, placed in the midst of something that neither time nor tide will ever erase.

Now it is common knowledge that early Christianity had problems with eros, and that the New Testament authors chose *agape* rather than *eros* to designate the love of God. They did this because they feared that the fleshly connotations of eros might blur the purity of God, the desire so prominent in eros might blur the self-sacrifice so prominent in Christ's cross. Both considerations are serious, and one cannot fault the New Testament authors' judgment. Eros alone lacks both the full light of the gospel and the gospel's defenses against selfishness. On the other hand, eros need not be alone. We can integrate it with agape, give it supplements of light and defense. When we do, the power of God moving in human attractions becomes so manifest that human attractions become not God's competitors but God's blessings.

Consider the alternative. If eros, in the energizing, transforming sense that we are using it, is not a blessing of God, then God seems the enemy of our very natures. The flame of eros comes from our human core. To demand that it be snuffed out in the name of the gospel would be to make the Christian God foolish (for having made us so erotic), or cruel (for so frustrating us), or suspect (for being so different from our spontaneous instincts). It makes much more sense, is much more in keeping with the God whose glory is human beings fully alive, to depict God as delighted when we flame forth in love, concerned only that we pursue this love generously enough, fully enough, to let it become as the mystics depict it, a living flame of purification, an inner ardor cleansed by the Holy Spirit.

When John comes aglow with desire for Mary and Mary reciprocates, they give the grace of God wonderful raw material. They are bursting with enthusiasm, energy, generosity. All things seem possible; nothing seems too hard or too costly. They want only to be good to one another, faithful to one another, worthy of one another. The shine in their eyes seems an eighth marvel of the world, the warmth in their hearts seems more precious than rubies. Like rockets about to be sent into orbit, they are building an initial thrust of enormous power, which will give them enough momentum for years of generous conjugal sharing. In due time their love will be tested. The years are sure to see to that. But good will demands that onlookers smile for them, and faith demands that onlookers thank God for another sign of the covenant.

Play

Once eros gains confidence that it is not foolish, it begins to loosen and play. Let Mary encourage John's ardor and John soon starts to strut his stuff. He has learned in childhood that play enlarges reality and incites creativity. Now he can learn that play also brings out further aspects of our personalities, as well as emotions quite like wonder and thanksgiving. So healthy lovers play to communicate further aspects of their talents, their hopes, themselves. Teasing, flirting, indulging in make-believe, they draw from one another wit and entertainment, share a growing little store of visions special to themselves. Of course sometimes they become silly or try too hard, but that is a small price for the growth their play offers, the outlet it gives their joy.

The spontaneous connections between eros and play bear notice for the sake of any marriage's future. If in their early relationship a couple learn to play well, in their later relationship play can easily reknit their affections, help them reenter the special, magical world they knew when first their eros was born. Since all relationships risk settling into overly practical routines, all relationships do well to think of providing play time. On the Sabbath, pious Jews traditionally have not only studied Torah and prayed in synagogue but enjoyed themselves and made love. On vacation, many couples have renewed their mutual enjoyment, refurbished their original romance and intrigue. The advertising industry, which tries mightily to exploit it, has made romance saccharine, but this abuse should not keep us from appreciating the Christian utilities of romance. Spouses need time together that is not just work or marital business. They need now and then simply to go to dinner, take a drive, slip away for a day at the beach. And they should not feel guilty at taking time for re-creation but realize that they are renewing the beauties of God's grace.

Sexual love is often at its best when it is playful, as we shall reflect in a section to come. Parenting can be at its most creative when it is playful, encouraging youngsters' squeals, sharing their imaginative expansion. The play of sports can free us from the grimness of work or service, laying out an arbitrary world of black and white that gives our frustrations clear targets. Even solitary exercise can become playful, once we get the body chugging. Then we can take on the role of a world-class miler, be for three or four laps of the pool Walter Mitty Spitz, hero of the 1972 Olympics. The play of exercise does many of its best services precisely by being unrealistic. Sending us back to the trenches unbent, refreshed, it makes concentration and sacrifice again possible.

So, too, with marital play, sexual or recreational. We know its quality not so much by the pleasure it brings in the doing as by its good effects later on. When the release of marital love brings no relief of daddy's distemper and helps mom's patience not at all, it is of questionable religious quality. When the evenings out for dinner do little for the mornings after of work and prayer, our relaxation is not fulfilling its purpose. That does not mean we should program our relaxations rigidly. It just means we should try harder to remember the heart of the Christian marital matter. In faith's perspective, two spouses should be growing into one more robust flesh. They should be growing more generative and wise. Play that stunts creativity or retards wisdom is less help than hindrance.

Is the Christian God playful? Can the followers of Christ take to heart the instinct of Hinduism that the Ultimate regards the world as somewhat amusing, a not unkind game or sport? Perhaps so. Since grace has abounded over sin and the resurrection dominated the crucifixion, the Christian story is essentially a comedy. At the deepest levels of the gospel, the news is surprisingly good. Thus the Roman Easter liturgy looks over the whole process of creation and redemption and exults, reaching such a pitch that it can look back on Adam's sin and call it a happy fault. Because it merited so great a redeemer and was the occasion for such a showing of love, even original sin, the root mystery of human depravity, can enter the song, be taken up into the play of a higher mystery. The Wisdom that played before God (Prov. 8:30), like a lithe maiden amusing a grave father or husband, knew the whole stretch of God's plan, and so worked the tragedy of human sin into the comedy of divine redemption. Where Aeschylus and the other Greek tragedians bemoaned the difficulty of fate, Dante and the other great Christian writers wondered at realms of purgation and paradise. After Christ, life no longer was hellish. A new story led beyond the grave, beyond despair, to undreamt realms of sweetness and light.

In their play, Christian spouses can exercise their faith in the resurrection, in Christ's triumph, in the ultimately comical character of history. Without denying the harsh aspects of workaday living, they can give themselves free zones in which to anticipate the fulfillment of heaven, enjoy the sacramentality of wine and bread.

Humor

Since Christian faith calls history a divine comedy, it finds laughter easy to come by. In the ultimate perspective of Christ's revelation, the evils that human beings perpetrate are more folly than deliberate vice. To be sure, one is hard put to see this on Calvary, or perhaps at any other time of suffering. Even when we can rise above the hurts we personally suffer, the hurts done to the innocent remain. Yet frequently the doers of evil *are* more foolish than diabolical. Frequently they are tripping on the hems of their egos, falling on the prats of their pride. Who can take seriously the pomp and bluster of the world's politicians, the furrowed brows of the military hawks? Their folly does lead to such awesome darknesses as nuclear stockpiles and worldwide famines. About its evil effects there can be no doubt. But in itself it is close to schoolyard tactics, silly taunts and childish shams. Looking at it with a little detachment demythologizes the gruesome enemy. Then Khrushchev and Nixon, Andropov and Reagan, seem but bit players in a second-rate farce.

Whatever utility such humor has for helping us gain perspective on international relations doubles for domestic turmoils. The ring in which we first learn how easily people lose perspective, how incongruous human animals frequently become, is the local family circus. There children rage about broken toys, parents rage about broken furniture, and no one rages about broken relationships. There teenagers spend more on pop music than books, parents spend more on doing than being. Everywhere, the household seems a little tilted, a little awry, as though a team of dwarfs kept shaking the foundation. One soon learns that the best way to right the balance is with the strong leverage of humor.

Of the humorists chronicling the incongruities of contemporary American marriage, Anne Tyler deserves special plaudits. Her novel *Morgan's Passing* so exaggerates oddities prevailing under many roofs that we recognize their funny parallels back home. Morgan Gower is a man of restless imagination who constantly tries on different costumes and roles. His long-suffering wife Bonny puts up with this patiently, because she knows it is more innocent than noxious. Morgan and Bonny are raising seven daughters, who keep changing under their eyes. Bonny largely accepts this but Morgan finds it bewildering. On good days it simply confuses him, but on bad days it makes him sad. Still, his sense of humor keeps frustrations from becoming destruction and in the bargain gives us a good model.

> The girls had taken over the kitchen by now. All of them were talking at once about history quizzes, boys and more boys, motorcycles, basketball games, who had borrowed whose record album and never given it back. A singer was rumored to be dead. (Someone said she would die herself if that were true.) Amy was doing something to the toaster. The twins were mixing their health-food drink in the blender. A French book flew out of nowhere and hit Liz in the small of the back. "I can't go on living here any more," Liz said. "I don't get a moment's peace. Everybody picks on me. I'm leaving." But all she did was pour herself a cup of coffee and sit down next to Morgan. "For heaven's sake," she said to Bonny, "what's that he's got on his head?"

"Feel free to address me directly," Morgan told her. "I have the answer, as it happens. Don't be shy."

"Does he have to wear those hats of his? Even in the house he wears them. Does he have to look so peculiar?"

This was his thirteen-year-old. Once he might have been offended, but he was used to it by now. Along about age eleven or twelve, it seemed they totally changed. He had loved them when they were little. They had started out so small and plain, chubby and curly and even-tempered, toddling devotedly after Morgan, and then all at once they went on crash diets, grew thin and irritable, and shot up taller than their mother . . .

He felt he was riding something choppy and violent, fighting to keep his balance, smiling beatifically and trying not to blink.

"See that? He's barefoot," Liz said.

"Hush and pour that coffee back," Bonny told her. "You know you're not allowed to drink coffee yet."

The youngest, Kate, came in with a stack of schoolbooks. She was not quite eleven and still had Bonny's full-cheeked, cheery face. As she passed behind Morgan's chair, she plucked his hat off, kissed the back of his head, and replaced the hat.

"Sugar-pie," Morgan said.

Maybe they ought to have another baby.[2]

Again and again, couples who prosper in their marriages do much of their coping with humor. Be it the trials of their kids, the worries of their bank accounts, or even the frictions between themselves, they manage to twist the data a half turn and make them comical. (This does not blind them to the similar binds and solutions being wrought by the neighbors next door. People who narrate their hilarious tales as though they alone scrape by on humor are tedious and strangely blinkered.) It suffices the well-adjusted couple to realize that progress on their home front almost always will entail accepting the Spirit's invitation to laughter, going with the sighs that relativize. It *is* funny that we should have expected thornless roses. It *is* ironic that our kids should be speaking to us as we used to speak to our parents. God must enjoy our Keystone Cop routines. The Parent of us all must have a broad sense of humor.

Warmth

The humor compatible with romantic eros and play is warm and kindly. Looking on the human comedy, it laughs in sympathy, not derision. In fact, we soon begin to question the humanity of those whose humor is cold or cutting. Quite likely, they are not in love with either God or a congenial spouse. The sad example of a poet we used to know comes to mind. Quite gifted at imagery and rhetoric, well-read and artistically refined, he used his talent coldly, cuttingly, to keep others subordinate or at bay. He could not abide the success of his colleagues. No other big frogs could frolic in his little pond. So, finding him less and less amusing, we grew more and more inclined to shun his company. Where faith might have made him attractively humble, exorcised his deep self-doubt, cynicism produced only weeds of brittle sarcasm, and self-concern led to more grimaces than belly laughs.

We should prize warmth, humor that brings a glow, in all our interactions, but perhaps especially in those on the home front. When spouses kid one another gently, warmly, they give voice to a sweet affection. So Bonny would blunt the girls' attacks on Morgan with little jokes of acceptance. So Ken can tell Barbie she's never been trimmer, it's the undies that keep shrinking. If Barbie knows her business, she can retort with but a glance at Ken's midriff. Then Ken will pull in his belly and tell four-year-old Katie the heroic story of how he first won her mother's heart. "I would eat up two or three of her scrawny little pies, Dumpling, and that would make her feel like the queen of the state fair." "Is that so, Mommy? Did you used to make scrawny little pies?" "If your daddy says so, dear. You can see how scrawny they made him." Then the dumpling will hit the daddy in the stomach, be punished by being hoisted in the air, and the whole family will embrace in laughter. Outsiders might find it silly, but the family trio find it rich food for love.

For the writer of the Epistles of John, the way we love one another ought to reflect the way God has loved us. Were a Christian family to reflect on this thesis, it might turn a spotlight on the value of warmth. First, there is the love of God poured forth in our hearts by the Holy Spirit. At memorable times, this has made our hearts burn within us. As we've followed the lessons of the scriptures, or sought Christ in the breaking of the bread, we've sensed how slow to believe cynicism has made us, how much we've resisted God's love. For the writer of the Gospel of John, Jesus wants to disclose to his followers all the secrets of his heart. He calls us friends not servants and kneels to wash our feet. The disciple whom he especially loves reposes on his breast at dinner, completely confident of his warmth. Through such details, the writer assures us of Jesus' affection. We do not follow a commanding officer but an intimate lover.

So it is with the spouse across our dinner table. Where prudence might counsel not expecting too much, settling for comfortable compatibility, faith counsels warming our love, letting God's love set us a higher ambition. Of course, if we do not associate warmth with religious love, if we have let our devotional lives run cold, the parallel will be uncompelling. Thus a Russian Orthodox monk once admonished a pilgrim visiting him:

> Yes, my friend, in our age of unbelief and carnal life we have become cold. Tears are considered a manifestation of pitiful weakness, something to be despised—good, perhaps, for old women, but no one else. On the other hand, a stony indifference and a hardness of heart are regarded as virility, self-possession, sangfroid. But, in truth, such an absence of tenderheartedness is merely a sign of spiritual death. A Byzantine mystic once said that those who go to Holy Communion without tears and a tender heart, and still more those who, celebrating the Holy Liturgy, remain stonily indifferent, all of them eat and drink the Body and

the Blood of the Lord unworthily. They are subject to condemnation. Therefore, cultivate tears and tenderness of heart, because only through them can we come to the purification of our thoughts. There is no other way.[3]

Is there another way to the maturity of one flesh than through warmth, affection, tears of sorrow, and tears of joy? Can the cold of heart ever inherit the riches of Christian espousal? The love of God that the monk touts takes the believer into a covenantal or marital religion. The beauty of God, the goodness of God, the forgiveness God has lavished upon us should move us to tears. Who are we, that God should have been so good to us? What right have mere human beings, finite and sinful, to such largess? When these emotions make us resolve to decrease our ego, so that we can increase our magnification of God, great quantities of fear fall away.

Granted, we marital partners are not good or gracious like God. Still, any marriage of depth or duration has seen much and forgiven more, been constant and often long-suffering. So marital love, too, can mingle the warmth of gratitude with the fire of desire. Fighting the good fight against coldness and isolation, it, too, can champion supple feeling.

Sexual Love

The eros, play, humor, and warmth that we have been considering are all species of sexual love, but it may profit us to spend a few pages explicitly on physical intimacy. Without taking on the graphic style of the medical manual, we want to make it clear that Christian marriage finds a powerful center in satisfying intercourse. Many problems are halved, if not solved, many enthusiasms spurred, if not doubled, when spouses regularly enjoy one another in bed. In fact, when spouses take on the disciplines necessary to assure good lovemaking on a regular basis, they are already working hard at the upkeep and improvement of their marriage. It doesn't require a decade of experience to bring home the lesson that good sexual love has definite preconditions and that our willingness or unwillingness to meet those preconditions is a telling index of the state of our marriage.

First, there is the crucial matter of time. We must make time for sexual love, set it high among our priorities. It must be time of high quality, when we are relaxed physically and have our minds at ease. There must be quiet and little danger of interruption. It helps mightily if the time before and the time after are compatible, further periods of leisure and intimacy. Probably fewer times of higher quality is better than more times of lower quality. Probably romantic leisure is more important than intense appetite. In Christian perspective, lovemaking is for repair, restoration, mutual fulfillment. It is the time when we sense that only united are we our full selves. Christian sexual love is much more than genital. It is the re-romancing of whole personalities, the rekindling of our full eros for the other's beauty of mind and soul, body and character. What times are most likely to aid such a blooming? When and where are we most apt to relax, see one another whole, recall the allure the other had when we were in our salad days?

Second, there is the matter of mood, which we have already insinuated. Now and then hormones combine with the phase of the moon to make for moods of urgency. The drive to couple, conquer or be taken, is so intense that subtlety leaves at the door. As the hymn writer might advise, praise God from whom such blessings flow. The energy flowing in our need testifies to God's biological power. By God's desire, the force of life feels strong, is compelling. This is the wisdom through which God keeps the species replenished, forces male and female to acknowledge their mutuality. Its simple starkness offers many occasions for laughter, lots of chances to tease and play. For example (before): "And what will you pay for such satisfaction, good sir? What will it profit me to spell you relief?" Or (after): "Now that that's out of the way, let's look into the monastic vocation. We have all the detachment it requires, don't you think, the freedom from carnal needs?"

Third, there is the matter of theology, strange as this may initially seem. Sexual intercourse would instruct us in the lessons of the Incarnation, making the love of God as penetrating and embracing as coitus. The way human bodies lean into one another, compress, caress, give and take is like the way God deals with us and the world. God romances us, seduces us, fulfills us on the model of sexual intercourse. Other models also apply, of course, and this model should not imply any strict need in God. But we can consider God's identification with us as bouncy, cuddly, ardent, relaxing, and ecstatic like marital intercourse. The play of spouses says a great deal about the play between Christ and the church. The loss of fear and gain of peace that comes through sexual love explains much about the Spirit, who romances the depths of our souls.

Fourth, there is the matter of bad times, when temporal, emotional, or physical forces cause us to misconnect. If the marriage is well grounded, somewhat advanced on its journey toward one flesh, these times will be almost trifling, something to laugh about. If the marriage is just stabilizing, or is under assault from other sides, these times may be serious and may sharply increase our frustration. Then any useful discussion will have to be very frank, entailing a hard look at our two bodies' evidence. Frank discussion is certainly preferable to avoidance or silence that stores up grudges, but the immediate moment may not be the best hour. Frequently it will be better to agree to a future discussion, in congenial circumstances, when the bruises have somewhat healed. Then it may be clear that pressures from the office, or pressures from the kids, or simple fatigue was the real bugbear. Then a single success can rout all the demons, bounce the marriage right back on the track.

CHAPTER

5

Commitment

Partnership

SEXUAL LOVE BOTH depends upon commitment and fosters it. Without commitment, sexual love is always on the verge of selfishness. With commitment, sexual love can build more commitment, as the fusion of two people, body and spirit, reaches out beyond itself, asking for further extensions and growth. Be these further extensions children or social service, they make sexual union a matter of not just private satisfactions but public contributions as well. One way to conceive of this expressive, outflowing side of sexual union is as a partnership.[1] As they are united physically, so the couple can conceive of themselves as united collaboratively for the work of their marriage, the adventure of their family, whatever confronts or rewards them.

Probably the key notion in a healthy marital partnership is justice or fair dealing. If the couple feel that their distribution of rights and duties, rewards and burdens, is fair, they likely will be able to work together, live together, peaceably. If one or both feel that the arrangement is unjust, that the stick has a short end, then the marital commitment has come under assault. It may survive, but it probably will not prosper. Few of us persist in carrying what we feel in our heart of hearts is an unfairly heavy burden without growing resentful. We may not express our resentment directly, but almost always it will escape in at least oblique ways. Monopolizing conversations, forgetting dates, mocking the other slightly in public, complaining passingly to the older children, refusing to play handyman, no longer fixing favorite dishes—the ways of getting back are legion. They are funny in novels or situation comedies, but in real life they cause much gnashing of teeth.

When, on the contrary, a partnership is clearly conceived and well executed, both parties usually chug along quite cheerfully. The quality of the conception and execution, of course, are primarily in the eyes of the couple themselves. Down the street from us Jane and Bill, mother of four and professional man, have a traditional distribution of work loads. He goes off to the office to earn the paycheck, she cares for the kids (ages six, four [twins], and two) and keeps house. They seem to have talked this through and decided that, at least for the present, this is the pattern that suits them. Later, when all the children are in school, she will look for work and pursue career interests of her own. Right now she is frazzled, her conversation a bubbly mass of non sequiturs, and her ego not a little assaulted. His job is not wholly satisfying, however, so they console themselves that their sufferings probably come close to balancing. What he must do to get them the basic financial support they need is equal to the frustrations she must handle running the family. On the weekends he is willing to take the kids off, work in the yard, and do some of "her" chores. During the week she is willing to shush the kids and amuse herself so he can have time and atmosphere to finish the work he sometimes has to bring home. They are partners, then: two people working out a common life, pulling together for common goals.

Another couple we knew some years ago seemed to have worked out a similar pattern but actually had not. To the embarrassment of all four of us, it came out in after-dinner conversation that the two of them had quite different notions of what their arrangement was. In his eyes, she ran the household and kept the kids shined up, because he was the one who could (by working very hard) gain them a quite affluent lifestyle. In her eyes, he worked so hard because he had to have a level of affluence that she could do without. She loved him and the children; she enjoyed the big house, nice car, good food, and the rest; but she would gladly have swapped a cutback in their standard of living for his being home more often and her having a chance to take a part-time job or go back to school. The tragic aspect of the situation was their discovery, after almost fifteen years of marriage, that they were working on two quite different sets of assumptions. As this became clear, unfortunately right out on the table in front of us, everyone realized that these two spouses had a sizable problem. They had collaborated to raise a family and keep things going, but without the clarity and contentment that might have been, without anything like a full partnership.

A childless couple provide still another view of partnership. Together they have worked out the careers they want, taking pains to make both careers subserve their life together. On one level, this has meant a choice for time over money. She, for instance, has decided not to accept administrative responsibilities that would have significantly raised her salary but probably also run her ragged. On another level, it has meant a choice for the kinds of work (teaching and art) that bring each of them the best combination of personal satisfaction and service to others. The marital benefit in this choice for works that bring out their best selves is a better interaction, a higher quality of personal sharing. Because each partner is able to focus on what he or she "ought" to do, each throws into the pot more joy, bounce, energy, playfulness, strength, etc. Their conversation is more interesting, their delight in good days is more soaring, and their satisfaction in bed is both more gracious and more fully referred to God.

Looking Forward

One rough-and-ready way to separate those who are well partnered from those whose partnership could use an overhaul is the direction in which the couple face. Well-partnered couples tend to look forward, enjoying today but leaning out to welcome tomorrow. Poorly partnered couples tend to blot out the future, losing themselves in the present or dredging up the past. In distinguishing themselves thus, the couples of course only mirror the ways that happy and unhappy people generally relate to time. To look forward to the future one must be hopeful, and to be hopeful one must find nature, society, one's self, and God gracious—realities more to be praised than feared. When nature seems wanton, or society seems crooked, or the self seems a failure, or God seems cruel, tomorrow looms as but more burdens and sufferings. For two people who have pledged themselves to share all of their tomorrows, the ability to hope is a sign that their pledge is paying off. Indeed, it is a sign of the working of God's pledge to them, the Holy Spirit who is God's down payment on our heaven.

To mend a partnership, therefore, we might stir up images of hope.[2] More concretely, we might become sufficiently playful and creative to reopen pathways that have become deadened, reconceive how we could make parenting or grandparenting or retirement attractive, alluring, a mixture of challenges and satisfactions. Maybe a good image would be working for a little cabin in the mountains or by the shore, where the whole family, or just the two of us, could get away for peace, quiet, and renewal. Maybe it would be subscribing to the symphony season and developing our love of music together. Politics could offer numerous possibilities, if we thought about getting the city council or the school board off their backsides. Prayer is nearly always relevant, for what could our marriage not become, were we to pray deeply and regularly together?

These images of ways two spouses could hope to do significant things together and so strengthen their partnerships are not meant to supplant their core common project of raising a family. What two people must do simply to put bread on the table and care for their kids is demanding almost to the point of exhaustion. But if the *élan* seems to have gone out of their bedrock collaboration, the sparkle to have fled, a new "outside" focus may revive it. This is especially the case if the two main zones of the bedrock collaboration, work and homemaking, are each almost exclusively the province of only one partner. In such a pattern, the overlap or intersection necessary for the *feeling* that we are working side by side may be hard to find. If he goes out "there," to the office or factory, to do his work, and she stays home "here," caring for a domain that he feels is only a little bit his, the division of labor is too strict to encourage a full partnership. Were she to do something in the work world, even if only on a part-time or volunteer basis, the work world would not seem alien to her or exclusively his. Similarly, were he to consider some portion of the house and family—the garden, the Sunday dinner, the kids' swimming meets—to be mainly his concern, the domestic sphere would not seem alien to him or exclusively hers.

The operative words in a good partnership are *we* and *ours*. Without making Jack and Jill clones, marital partnership would mold them to think of their money, property, kids, community service, and very lives as things thoroughly shared. It is a sign of marriage's being alive and well that so many American couples do develop this sense of community. Partly by choice and partly by the inevitable effects of living under the same roof, they do have more and more difficulty distinguishing where one begins and the other leaves off. This is not a dangerous or immature submersion of one personality in another, a loss of the independence necessary for adulthood, successful parenting, spouseship, or solid work. It is a freely accepted working of marital time, in which tie after tie of shared pain, joy, dullness, or delight binds the couple together. It is her working in the yard in one of his old shirts, cute in the way it swamps her. It is his reading her books and using her lines quite willing to credit the source. With the kids, it is the interchangeability possible at many ages, when either parent can be chauffeur, bedtime storyteller, hugger, or bottom smacker. With the church, it is her showing up to teach his Sunday school class when he has laryngitis, his bringing the cake for the bake sale when she has to work late at the office.

People willing to use their wits and stir up their sense of adventure will easily think up a dozen ways to look forward positively. The plays we might see, the vacations we might have, the good works we might perform in the neighborhood or at church are virtually infinite. The limits of our marriages are the limits of our imaginations. The way we face the future is essentially in our own hands. Yesterday is gone (though we can retrieve it for comfort and forgiveness). Today is the time of decision and opportunity. Tomorrow is the child of today, the fruit by which we may judge today's decisions. If today we hear God's voice summoning us to quicken our marital hopes, stir up our sense of marital adventure, let us harden not our hearts. For pleasure and service, let us put our heads together, join hands, and find things we want to do, goals we want to reach, rich dividends our partnership might pay.

Keeping Faith

We may think of commitment as a partnership that leans into the future hopefully. If they can concern themselves with things they want to accomplish together, a couple can grow closer and closer almost unthinkingly. A positive momentum is on their side, and they need merely keep the wheels turning. Still, the life of faith profits greatly from reflection, for only in reflection do we give ourselves the chance to discern the patterns of our onward movement, listen for the changes the Spirit might be proposing. If we are all doing, with no reflecting, we thin out our being, forget the height and depth and breadth of the love of God in which grace would immerse us. Then our commitment becomes less a pledge to God and our spouse than a series of useful but not especially religious work habits. The weeks race by absorbingly, but the core of our marriage goes hungry.

Reflecting on commitment, one finds that Christian marriage only comes into its own when its partnership is a matter of keeping and expanding faith. We must nourish both faith in God and faith in one another, or our marriage will not shine with Christ's luster. The faith we keep with God is covenantal, our trust that God walks with us through our life cycles. This faith is liveliest when we refer all times, good and bad, to God's providence, offering praise in the morning and regrets by the light of the stars. It is flabby, in need of rejuvenation, when we live as though God made no difference, were a completely silent partner. That was not the faith of Abraham, the father of all biblical believers, nor the faith of Jesus and Paul. To keep the faith of the New Testament, we must have a lively assurance of the things we hope for (Heb. 11:1), a quick reference of both joy and suffering to God. If God is not giving us this day our daily bread and forgiving us our trespasses, God is not really functioning as our father.

The faith we keep with our spouse reposes on this faith in God, but it has its own peculiar province as well. Usually it begins when we are but rose-lipped maidens and light-footed lads, to borrow from the poet A. E. Housman. The beauty for which we first grow erotic is like an overture to the full marital symphony our love is begging to unfold. If we let it, by working at keeping faith, this beauty will return at steady intervals, always with slightly different overtones or harmonies, but still discernibly the same. The lips may somewhat pale with age, the feet grow somewhat heavy, but now and then a smile in the sunroom or a hop to the curb will bring back the early beauty. Even more, the later beauty, less apparent but more substantial, will fulfill the early promise, giving eros satisfactions it could not suspect when first it came to flame.

Spouses keep faith when they hold to the vision that first flamed up in their souls. This holding is not rigid or grasping. It admits of change, evolution, and even some discontinuity. But overall it allows the couple to say that they have pretty much steered the course they first set out upon, largely fulfilled their pledge to try to keep moving forward through good times and bad. The faith, like the relationship and the spouses themselves, may have nicks and bruises, scars and wrinkles. Some of its hardiness will show in its having weathered storms, pains, sufferings. The sort of peace that comes after the battle can't be anticipated before the battle. The sense of confidence and reliability that comes after decades of testing can't be generated at the outset by mere wishing.

What, though, about infidelity, which is the opposite of keeping faith? Perhaps a case study will best serve to answer. Once (would that it were only once) a man in his early forties half-thinkingly stumbled into an affair with a woman at least a dozen years younger. Since the man, whom we'll call Samuel, was married, it was a matter of infidelity to the point of adultery. Since the man was long married—almost twenty years—it was a serious matter, a contradiction of what more than 7,000 days and nights of living together had assumed, rested upon, and seemed to be forwarding. Samuel was half-thinking in this affair, because to be full-thinking would have made it unlikely, well-nigh impossible. He had to shut off part of his brain, drug part of his conscience, distract himself with what others in the fast track were doing. He could not do this with integrity, of course, and when the mess hit the fan he saw himself as a betrayer. But while he was escaping for pleasure and dalliance he didn't feel very bad; indeed, the flow of his hormones pumped him up, made him feel ten years younger.

When his wife, whom we'll call Sarah, discovered the situation, she was very deeply hurt. For reasons we shall go into in the next section, she could not take the adultery as just another instance of male menopausal madness or just another instance of human sinfulness become painfully concrete at home. Rather it slashed at the core of her bond to the man, chilling her affection to the source. In the lengthy discussions, counseling sessions, and repair projects that followed, Samuel and Sarah finally faced problems they had long neglected and got a much clearer picture of themselves. But when last we saw them it was still in doubt whether they would be able to recapture the trust they had once had. Ruefully, they were learning that faith not actively kept is faith perilously close to being lost.

Forgiveness

In the Christian scheme of things, God offers us forgiveness as a way to handle our sins. Without minimizing our objective guilt, letting us ignore the harm our sins do to either others or ourselves, God allows us to return at any moment, like the amazingly good father of Luke 15. The church has institutionalized this aspect of the good news by sacramental rites or less formal services that would mediate contrition, forgiveness, and penance.[3] Seventy times seven, the biblical hyperbole has it, we should forgive the neighbor who comes to confess her wrong, reknit the tattered relation. This does not mean we can refuse the neighbor when the count reaches 491. It means that even if we take the number that designates fullness (7), multiply it by 10 and then multiply that by fullness again, we won't have exhausted the depths of God's graciousness. God's forgiveness is but another facet of God's being and love. For God to be God means that whenever a creature opens itself God stands ready to repair and give again.

This seems a wonderful model, a golden archetype, until it comes to forgiving our enemies. It is hard enough to beg forgiveness when we know we have wronged another. It can be excruciating to feel bound to forgive an enemy who yesterday was breathing hate in our face. The enemy has hurt us so badly that forgiveness seems cheap grace, a facile ploy, an evasion of justice and truth. And, of course, some petitions for forgiveness are just that: further condemnations of the petitioner. But Jesus' profoundly simple wisdom comes to our aid here, as in so many social situations. Our Christian calling is to love our neighbors as we love ourselves. Unless we are pathological, we come to terms with our own failings, let go of the recriminations we bear our worse selves, and get on with the business of living. Only the neurotically rigid or self-punishing among us do not finally give themselves a boot in the rear and resume the friendship between the outer and inner parts of their personalities.

For marriage, the most intimate of personal relationships, forgiveness obtains with special acuteness, because the "enemy" is the one we had expected to play the leading roles of lover and best friend. On the small stage are the daily irritations that humor usually forgives somewhat wryly. Once again, Anne Tyler has depicted with wicked accuracy the way things are in many households:

> The first time Harley kissed me, he had to brush off this bedspread before-hand that we'd been sitting on. Wouldn't you think that might have told me something? Every night now before he goes to sleep he perches on the edge of the bed and brushes off the soles of his feet. These bare white feet, untouched... what could have dirtied them? He wears shoes every waking moment and slippers if he takes one step in the night. But no, there he sits, so methodical, so exact, everything in its proper sequence, brush-brush... sometimes I think I'll hit him. I'm fascinated, I stand there watching him brush his left foot first, his right foot second, not letting either touch the floor once he's finished with it, and I think "I'm going to bash your head in for you, Harley."[4]

Jenny, the speaker, does not bash in the head of Harley, her husband, but she does finally divorce him. They cannot reconcile his over-orderliness with her harum-scarumness, find a higher viewpoint from which to forgive one another their irritating habits. In the case of Samuel and Sarah that we considered in the last section, forgiveness became a blockbuster production, because Samuel took a long time to confess the wrong he had done, while Sarah fell into a deep crisis of self-image. Samuel was slow to feel guilty because the adulterous affair had been the most energizing, emotionally charged experience he'd had in years. Previously locked into a strong sense of duty, he had used the affair to break out to a less inhibited, freer, more playful self. Sensing this, and taking it as an attack on her own adequacy as a lover, Sarah felt doubly betrayed. The scenario seemed to be becoming a case of "blaming the victim," the one already battered and bruised. In addition, Sarah's upbringing had made her both shy about sex and rigidly scornful of permissive mores. So she dug in her heels and dramatized her victimhood, steadily losing sympathy among the many friends and counselors she burdened with her unending tale. She could not let the episode slip into the sorry but long line of Christians' sins and infidelities. It had to keep playing as tragedy number one, prime-time heartbreak and crisis.

Somewhere between permissiveness and hardness of heart lies a golden mean called Christian forgiveness. To help Samuel and Sarah reach it, the wisest of their friends (older and better visioned) finally insisted that it was time to get the train moving, the journey back under way. The couple had themselves stuck in Dullsville, Guiltsburg, far off the Christian main line. If Samuel was sincere in saying he wanted to repair the marriage, recoup the past and regenerate the future, he had to foreswear his adolescent regressions and work on making his eros adult. If Sarah really wanted to remain his wife, she had to call his clay clay, not nuclear radiation, and relearn the truth that carnal failings mean less than deep spite. To their credit, Samuel and Sarah did finally forgive and get moving again. We pray that their faith is now in better keeping.

Realism

Occasionally the philosopher Immanuel Kant would pose his studies in terms of apparently quite simple questions. One such key question was, "What may we hope?" It comes to mind here, because the bottom line in any Christian reflection on commitment might well be, "What is realistic? What may spouses sanely ask, expect, hope from one another?" The expectations of American culture are now quite minimal, as divorces equal surviving marriages. The symbols of Christian tradition are breathtakingly idealistic, shining like the gold and rubies of that city set high on a hilltop, the new Jerusalem. Is realism, like virtue, somewhere in the middle? Can commitment mature and not make us wimps? Jesus probably expected fidelity and loyalty from the twelve he had tutored, yet at the end he was completely alone. The women at the cross were some consolation, but far too few and too late. Knowing the human heart, how would Jesus counsel two young partners? What would Jesus' sober realism likely be?

Jesus consorted, by preference, with whores and tax collectors, some of the prime sinners of his day. We may be sure he did not do this because he found their shadowy world attractive, was intrigued by their aberrations or excesses. No, Jesus went out to sinners such as these because they were especially needy, especially despised by the establishment, and therefore especially open to his radically new message. The main defenses we erect against God's love are habit, propriety, and privilege. As long as our ruts take us pleasurable places, we are not likely to detour. As long as we sit with the gilded and praised, we are not likely to support a revolution. The sinners of Jesus' day sometimes knew how desperately the kingdom of God was needed. The Pharisees and priests of Jesus' day seldom did. So Jesus turned sinfulness into fertile ground. In one of those blessed transformations that comprise the grand sweep of redemption, he made forlornness and moral breakdown occasions of grace.

What has all this to do with marital realism? If Jesus' treatment of sinners, as his treatment of human beings generally, is our guide, it is realistic to hope that people will be open to grace. Thus, it is realistic to hope that couples will keep seeking and finding God's overtures. It is also realistic not to be surprised that people sometimes miss the mark, forget their calling, stumble, and come up soiled. Thus, it is also realistic not to be surprised when one's partner shows imperfections—on occasion is grouchy, spendthrift, boastful, or lustful. Finally, it is realistic to believe in God's regenerative powers: grace that heals, sacraments that forgive, people who can forgive seventy times seven. Thus, finally, it is realistic to believe that spouses can forgive one another, mend their fractured feelings, absorb hurts and infidelities into stronger faith and love.

The realistic person doesn't presume to predict what any free agent will do. Such a person knows the range of human capabilities and is aware of the statistical medians around which human performances hover but also refuses to play prophet or God. People want to do what is right, love the beauty of God's plan, but are easily distracted. In a pinch they can be extraordinarily generous, but most days laziness and selfishness divert them. One should neither expect sin nor be surprised at its steady occurrence. One should take each day as a fresh gift from God, another time God can make all things new, wipe away every tear from our eyes.

If we take this back to Samuel and Sarah, thrashing his infidelity and her bitterness once more, we may conclude that the most realistic analysis finds their pain occasioning their further growth in faith. In retrospect, looking for how God might have been writing straight with crooked lines, we see that Samuel's upswing of testosterone was but a superficial symptom. Locked into an immature

personality structure, so rigid he was running on obligation and willpower alone, Samuel came to the point where
"God" was but part of an oppressive superego, a conscience too heavy to bear. The realism of his hunger was
the realism of Nietzsche: any true God must dance and
sing, be full of life and passion. The unrealism, the cruelty,
was his self-serving assumption that his wife could never
be passionate, that he alone knew the meaning of spring.

The unreality in Sarah's outlook showed in the degree
of her shock and trauma. As though she had been living in
a bunker, she treated the adultery as an utter novelty. As
though her Christian perfection had put her beyond all
possibility of failure, wrapped her in impregnable lacquer,
she could not admit their marriage might be troubled. So
Sarah fled to legalism and finally was shattered. Picking
up the pieces was a very painful way to learn humility, but
ultimately a blessing, for now her God can be mysterious,
not just a tidy notion. Now God can point the way to real
progress, cast out her worst fears. Tomorrow Sarah may be
a woman who can bend, gaze clear-eyed, cry honestly, and
love till she overflows.

CHAPTER

6

Work

Creativity

WHEN FREUD COINED his famous summary of the requisites of mental health, the abilities "to love and to work," he spotlighted the two drives that have seemed to many psychologists most central. Christians, in light of Jesus' twofold commandment, might want to round things out by referring to the prayer that is a large part of our love of God and the political service that is a large part of our love of neighbor, but they can work comfortably with Freud's terms. For Christians, too, ought to be mightily concerned with the forces that make for health, growth, progress, and productivity. No less than good pagans taught by the wise man from Vienna, we should realize that work places itself before us and our contemporaries as a prime ingredient of our happiness or sadness. Not to appreciate this would be to misunderstand one of the most powerful forces in any marriage. The two trying to become one flesh either contend with work or settle for being one skin.

The godlike portion of work is its creativity. Just as there is an overwhelming eros that makes us ecstatic for the beauty of another human being, so there is an overwhelming eros for beautiful work. Probably we see this most clearly in artistic work, but many kinds of labor aspire to it. For the scientist it may be the vision of a perfect explanation, in the service of which all the antiseptic laboratories and computers have been toiling. For the honest businessman it may be a more efficient organization and so an almost elegant customer service. The politician can aspire to the beautiful sight of people come together, cooperating, filling with rightful pride at the potential of their community. The pastor may labor to achieve a perfect Sunday morning, when the children sing like angels and the grace of the Lord would stir a wooden bench. The housewife can yearn for a spotless kitchen that epitomizes a spotless home, unsmudged by fear, pain, or resentment.

We each have our visions, great or small, and we work by the glow of their love. They tell us our time is for making, creating, bringing into being things that were not. Few other species have this capacity. We ourselves only learned it through millennia, perfecting the thumb and larynx necessary for manipulation and communication, developing the frontal lobes that process the memories, sense impressions, and abstractions necessary to flash forth new forms. Because of this evolutionary accomplishment, and the plethora of things we can now sculpt, it is not utter conceit to call ourselves images of God, like to our source in being makers. In the beginning, God made the heavens and the earth. In the end, God will make a new heaven and a new earth. In the middle, we chip and plot and ponder, trying to fashion a history that might be worth making new.

The home in which work is creative ought to count itself peculiarly blessed. The world over, many homes house people worn down by drudgery, or people grateful for any sort of work. Even in our affluent nation, those who do fulfilling work seem scarcely a fraction of those bored and frustrated. As Studs Terkel, the famous chronicler of ordinary people, quotes one of his interviewees: "I think most of us are looking for a calling, not a job. Most of us, like the assembly line worker, have jobs that are too small for our spirit. Jobs are not big enough for people."[1] Since our country does not define itself as seeking work that would ennoble people, jobs are bound to be somewhat inhumane. The face of mammon is not beautiful. (It

would be the task of a Christian economics to improve it.)
Thus, those who do love their work, can call it beautiful,
ought to thank their God every night.

On the way to such a prayer, spouses do well to talk
things through thoroughly. Fortunately, many have this
instinct and courage. When one or the other is not happy
at work, the whole household suffers. It may take more
guts to face this, and its deep-going implications, than to
plod along year after year. We saw this recently (and
somewhat paradoxically) in the case of two friends, both
lawyers, who had moved to take what looked like an ideal
job. He would get out of the rat race, no longer have to
fashion briefs for energy barons. She would go back to
school and broaden her competence for divorce work, in
which clinical psychology seemed as important as law. But
the man with whom he was going to apprentice picked up
and left precipitously. That meant no training to meet
daunting responsibilities, and within six weeks our friend
was in way over his head.

Thus when his old bosses approached him about coming
back, the family decided they should accept the offer.
Blush as they would to turn up at friends' doors four
months after having left forever, they felt the new job
would have given him an ulcer and made the rest of them
miserable. They had to get out from under. Returning to
the old job was hardly the Hollywood script they would
have written, but it seemed the wise, moral choice. So
they are back in our midst, rueful but happier. They have
learned a great deal about work, and it has made them
more compassionate. Were we to ask them for six months
in which to go crazy, they would grant them with a grin.

Money

The creativity of work directly affects our spiritual lives.
The money received for work affects our spiritual lives
indirectly. We must work for money, unless we are a very
rare breed. For most of us, as for Adam, bread comes by

the sweat of our brow. This need not so link work with original sin as to cast a dark shadow over all labor. Human toil is dour enough without burdening it with direct sinfulness. In the light of Christ's cross, the better way is to regard human labor as a major vehicle of God's redemption. Willy-nilly, we stretch out our arms and imitate our Savior, pushing body and mind to make a living. If we accept this necessity in good cheer, we let God be a stern but thorough teacher. Throwing aside the playboy ideal, the soft life dangled by a sugar daddy, we stand with Jesus and Paul, who were ordinary working men. Where they planed wood and sewed tents, we may punch computers or set bones, but the differences are relatively minor. They toiled for their keep, and we remain able to understand them.

At its best, then, money is an honest token of solid toil. At its worst, it is the root of most of our evils. Jesus tried to teach us this in several ways, but perhaps most strikingly in the parable of the grumbling workmen (Matt. 20:1–16). As you recall, various workmen are hired at different times throughout the day, so they expect different wages at quitting time. When the employer gives those who worked the most what he promised them, but also gives the same amount to those who worked the least, the ones hired early start grumbling. The employer rebukes them, pointing out that if he chooses to be generous it is no skin off their noses. The main implication of the parable is the uncalculating generosity of God, who treats us far better than we deserve, but a secondary point is the ungodliness of becoming grasping about money. Only the heathen chase after riches and pleasures. Children of God have a higher calling.

In too many troubled marriages, this higher calling has ceased to echo. Swept into the currents of the culture at large, children of the light can begin to chase dark fancies. What begin as innocent desires to improve the house, or put a little dash in the wardrobe, or spruce up the car gain a driving hunger of their own. Then more and more acquisitions mean less and less freedom until the family revolves around its possessions. The money to polish all this glitter becomes terribly important and soon comes the question, "Is there life after Mastercard?" Having helped several sets of friends through bankruptcy, we think we see a recurring pattern. When their star falls back to earth, the couple discover they haven't been prayerful for quite some time. In the beginning they were lean and hungry, like the Baptist and the Christ. Slowly they became soft fat cats. Fat cats don't inherit God's kingdom, so the harvest mainly brings sadness.

At another level of faithlessness there are false prophets who manipulate many. The sizable number of Christians, both mainstream and evangelical, who thump about money and suggest that the pious will wax fat are inbred and feebleminded. One has only to look at Jesus' life and fate to know that profiteering preachers, bishops, or elders are hypocrites of the first order. You can't fulfill Jesus' first command in anything remotely resembling the way he himself fulfilled it and turn out a lover of money. You can't hear Jesus' second command, look at the world's one billion malnourished, and in good conscience thrust your snout in the trough. No one has the right to luxuries as long as anyone lacks necessities. That is traditional Christian social teaching, and those who flout it today open the doors to bloody revolutions.

In our domestic go-rounds with money, we had best get our heads screwed on straight. We need enough money to live simply and freely, to avoid want and school our kids. Beyond that, our piles of money court spiritual loss, the wasting of our faiths. The list of things that feed the Christian spirit—prayer, study, sympathy, service, love, art, science, parenting—need not mention money till the eighth or ninth place. At their best, Christians, like Muslims, strengthen the spirit by giving their money away. At one and the same time, both help people less fortunate than themselves and restrain their own acquisitiveness. If the enclaves of privilege in our midwestern city are representative, without such restraint acquisitiveness soon grows cancerous.[2] Two miles away people despair of getting work, weep at the sight of their kids' rags. Down the street neighbors nibble *delices de France* and talk about how the poor rip off the successful. The money that keeps such people from seeing how things really are, what is actually going on, is the deepest enemy of their souls. Without it they would be in the common struggle, feel the common stings, know why God had better hasten. With it they have eyes but do not see, ears but do not hear. Even God is hard put to move them.

Service

One strong antidote to letting money dictate one's work, and through one's work one's family life, is the creativity we mentioned earlier. If an eros for making something beautiful directs our labor, money will stay secondary. A second strong antidote is service, and it has impeccable biblical credentials. People who conceive of their work as love of their neighbors, aid to their neighbors' bodies, minds, or spirits, are not likely to be co-opted by mammon or trivialities. Human beings have so many genuine, even raw and bleeding needs that working to produce trivialities seems a terrible waste of time. Even in our own country, to say nothing of the world, huge needs for food, clothing, housing, medical care, and education cry out for speedy treatment. Millions live on the streets, a sidewalk register their furnace. Some thirty million citizens live below the poverty line, and God knows how many illegal aliens. The official figures on unemployment, which tell far less than the whole story, show that a majority of black youth are unemployed. The steady escalation of medical costs puts the elderly in deep anxiety. Yet distraction and self-indulgence glow with health, gilding the ads of *The New Yorker*. No wonder Christ must lament liturgically each year, "My people, what have I done to you? In what have I affronted you? Answer me!"

We cannot answer. Sin never makes any sense. Given the world's wealth of resources, we choose to squander, make war, and pollute. The problem is not nature's bounty, the opportunities the Creator provides. The problem is humanity's blindness, our constant refusal to share. Until we find motivations better than money, more moving than material gain, the world will continue in peril. Christian service only assumes its full significance when we set it in these ultimate perspectives. Much of the service that is most pressing is work we shouldn't have to do, repairs required by human folly.

"O well," you may say, "that is just the human condition." You could not be more wrong. There is no necessity in any particular stupidity or sin, as there was no necessity in the stupidity of Pilate, the sin of Iscariot. If we are not puppets, do have a real freedom, our wreckage is our own doing. Too many people justify their laziness or the disorders of the world on the basis of an ill-considered "human nature." In a caricature of Luther and Calvin, too many write other people off as selfish curs and double the guard round their own castles. In their own eyes, they are the elect, prosperous and mannered, wise for doubting the motivations of others. In fact they are murderers of community who bring tears to the prophets' cheeks. You can't make progress until you believe progress is possible. You can't believe progress is possible if your view of human nature renders bridge-building or creativity or self-sacrifice unthinkable.

Consider the two following examples, and decide which one's work is servant. Churchgoer A is a physician working in family practice. His fees are moderate. If you've got big troubles or worries, you can see him in twenty-four hours. He loves his work and has hands that heal. He doesn't say much about his philosophy of medicine. He won't let you take him out to lunch. He's shy, almost awkward, outside his consulting rooms. That's where he can make you happier, lighten your burdens, so from there he's not easily moved. He doesn't do dramatic surgery. He's happy to heal a boil or a wart. He's made many lives discernibly less anxious, so he turns up regularly in many prayers.

Churchgoer B is a teacher, a formal type not much given to humor; and although she has joined an idealistic profession she doesn't think of her studies or lectures as a service. The students who pay her salary are but an unfortunate necessity, a platform for her forwarding of Truth. They could never grasp her intricacies, her rich spin of implications, but times are hard so she has to put up with them, rubbing their noses in "real" education. One doesn't find B around the office much, nor on many committees. When she has accomplished her minimal duties, she makes a beeline back to her study. There she puts on Wagner and returns to occupations worthy of her superior intellect. From time to time little bits of writing emerge, packaged off to esoteric journals. A few get published, more do not, but B's vigor seldom slackens. It is not the public to whom she looks for reward. It is not even God. (B's church is more social than religious.) It is the tiny committee of competent peers who appreciate "frontier" work.

This is not exactly an untilted comparison, in which the contrast between service of others and service of self would remain somewhat subtle. As the descriptions took shape on our page, B grew less and less sympathetic. Cold, arrogant, and closed, she works only for herself. A, on the other hand, is a man of constant giving, a model hard to overpraise. Having chosen a work that could pivot on money, he never lets money intrude. Although he could squirrel away his riches and please himself, his patients always have a claim upon him. He is ministerial, servant, selfless down to his quick and marrow. So the angel writes his works in gold and wishes he'd take B aside. She doesn't labor for money, but her pride constantly does her in. Where she could be a profitable servant, she's more like a useless queen.

Compromise

There is a line in the last section that may have stuck in some craws: "His patients always have a claim upon him." Transposed for the teacher, business executive, pastor, or other worker, it may have rung sour in more than a few spouses' minds, set up some bad vibrations. In some households ministerial (servant) work can seem the enemy of family life. Spouses can be so taken up with outside responsibilities, so diligent in helping customers or clients, that their family feels neglected or ill-used. That does not seem to be the case with the physician we described, whom we see with his wife and daughter at the symphony. In his arrangement of his time and services, he clearly provides for recreation and home life. Apart from emergencies, which can of course occur, he locks the door firmly against overwork, refuses to become a workaholic.

We shall develop the implications of such a refusal in the next section, where we consider the benefits of a Sabbath. Here the conflicts between work and family life bid for our attention. How can a couple develop a compromise between what they owe one another and their kids and what they owe, or at least want to serve, the people they deal with at work? What formula might lay things out clearly, for the peace and quiet of all? Well, we've yet to come across a simple formula, much as we'd encourage anyone to search. The needs of both the given family and the given people they serve can vary considerably. Psychologists can pinpoint critical stages in children's development, when a move or inattention would be especially dangerous. A business can go through trying times, when all hands have to work extra shifts. Special financial burdens caused by illness or education can force a spouse who had been home to take an outside job. There can be few fixed formulas, only a couple of general rules.

First, we think that a couple do well to talk through their loves for and responsibilities to both their home lives and their work. Despite all the energy these two focuses demand, many couples never correlate them clearly. In such talk, our bias is in favor of family life. Ideally work and family life integrate smoothly, and there is no denying that spouses unhappy in their work have a tougher time at home. But sometimes work and family life are on a collision course and spouses have to decide which is their greater treasure. Academic life now harbors a surprising number of couples who live apart so that each spouse can have a career. We don't want to be judgmental, but this seems a poor recipe for a Christian marriage. For brief periods it might be necessary, or for a few exceptional personalities. In most cases it more likely represents a failure of imagination or compromise, or it is the death knell of the marriage.

Second, having expressed our preference for the rights of the home over the rights of the office, we would promote the search for creative compromises. People who have talents that they need to use, and that would profit society, ought to keep juggling the pieces until something viable falls out. Maybe the place won't be ideal, or the time or the money, but by persistence one will be able to make a worker's contribution, which is the heart of Christian economics. If the pressures come from the other end, from too much work rather than too little, the family will have to go into council and decide how to cut back, what they will sacrifice to spend more time together. If faced with a promotion, they may decide they don't want to move, or work twice as hard, or take on harrowing responsibilities. Whatever threatens to rob a family of the amount of quality time they need to be a circle of love looms as their enemy. Having a clear agreement on their priorities greatly helps to cut this enemy down to size.

The majority of cases, of course, involve compromising in our emotions as much as in our decisions. For example, our friends who just moved from Kansas to Pennsylvania, because his job in Kansas was shutting down and a good new job opened in Pennsylvania, regretted the move but had little realistic alternative. The kids lamented leaving their schools and friends but soon saw that it had to be. The parents did their best to buffer the bumps but the entire family suffered. They wisely put most of their energy into handling their blues and their most recent letters have turned upbeat. In another case that we saw recently, a couple decided against her pushing for a big promotion. When they looked at the changes the promotion would entail, they decided it wasn't worth it. Their longtime standard had been "time over money" and by that standard they would have been stepping backwards. As long as they had enough money to live as free spirits they could do without the promotion.

So our third suggestion for compromise would be that in conflicts between time and money, time ought to get the benefit of the doubt. The months race by quickly enough without mortgaging more of them. One's lover grows gray and one's kids shoot up; album after album fills. Will a bigger car or a sharper television set replace the picnics and lovemakings that slipped away? Will thicker rugs and heavier meals compensate for prayer, music, reading, and quiet talk that might have been richly shared? Not many Christian spouses think so, in times of sanity or faith. The main lines of many compromises are plain enough, like the relations of God to mammon.

The Sabbath

Those who saw the musical *Fiddler on the Roof* perhaps remember the Sabbath song. Like many parts of the musical, it grew from the memories of eastern European Jews recorded in the book *Life Is with People*.[3] When those Jews summarized the three treasures of their traditional faith, they spoke of Torah, marriage, and good deeds. When they recalled their best celebrations, they spoke of the blessed Sabbath days, when God's rest came adorned like a bride for her Lord. This was mythological talk, of course, picturesque speech to portray God's mysteries boldly. But it lent the right aura to the moment that Sabbath began, when the mother would shield her eyes and light the Sabbath candles. From that moment at sundown to sundown of the next day, there was to be no work or sadness. This was God's day, holy time, when the goodness of being Jewish ought to flower. So people ate the special meal (several days in preparation) with gusto and gratitude. They went out of their way to be kind to the stranger in their midst, brought in to share in the joy. They studied the Torah and went to the synagogue, remembering their faith, their God, and their ancestors. Parents tried to entertain their children and find rest and lovemaking for themselves.

No doubt we would profit from analyzing the Sabbath on any of several levels, but its greatest relevance here is the light it sheds on work. When they keep a Sabbath, people teach themselves that their work is not their life. Fulfilling or necessary as their work may be, it is much less than their whole selves, much less than their God's whole requirement of them. To be all work and no rest or recreation would be to live like a robot. To make all days the same would be to thin time to utter profanity. The things that work doesn't cover—contemplation, aesthetics, rest, and play—are as important as what it does. If we would make a limitation on work just one day a week, we would do wonders for our religious spirits.

It is not enough, of course, merely to stay home from the office. A weekend packed with but other species of busyness is not what biblical religion calls a Sabbath. On the other hand, the images bequeathed us by the Pilgrims (the man who would clout you if you slumped in church) are also not helpful. You don't get rest and recreation of spirit, refresh your joy and deepen your peace, by legalistic rigors, more hard patches of willfulness. When church becomes as dutiful as business, Sunday is the butt of the week.

No, another attitude is called for, something unpragmatic and free. The Sabbath should mainly be time that is

unco-opted—leisure, holism, and grace. Leisure not only
empowers culture (and at the center of culture is cult:
nonprofit worship of God), it guards us against neurosis.
You can't run a Sabbath like a factory. Management by
objectives doesn't hold. A Sabbath is for waiting on the
Spirit, turning one's face to the breeze. The breeze blows
where it will. On the Sabbath we can search and follow it.
We can flow with the breeze full time.

So there is good counsel against filling the Sabbath with
organized projects or games. Better a spontaneous swim
party or softball game than more Girl Scouts or Little
League. Certainly a no to dull guests, who would take
away the family's recreation. As in many other cases, the
trick lies in the discernment. It is more how we do things
than what they entail. It is the spirit of unhurried immersion rather than the spirit of seizing the day. Things that
ease the mind are better than things that stir the blood. A
good touchstone is the closeness of prayer. When the sky
opens up, the soul centers down, the Sabbath mood is
near. When God would intrude or Jesus would be out of
place, the Sabbath has slipped away.

This implies that mature Christian prayer can be
comfortable, is not always stiff or constrained. If we cannot
pray at the beach or the mountains, we'd best overhaul
our understanding of prayer. Adolescents may have to
work these things out slowly, threading their way through
complex circuits. Adults are ill-served indeed if they reach
forty and know nothing of contemplation.

Contemplation is the ability to attend: be present, stay
open, admire, and enjoy. With but the slightest twist of
focus, it can become prayer like the psalmist's. The ever-
lasting hills—why have I not noticed them for weeks? The
vivid green of the annual rye—what painter could mix its
equal? There goes Molly, braids flying—how wonderful
her health and vigor. Is that fresh bread I smell through
the window, stirring thoughts of wine and thou?

*Dear God, the profusion of things in which you come to
us! Truly are you a God of people, a worker of sacraments.*

Whenever I have eyes to see, you show me hues I never noticed. Whenever I have time to collect my parts, you whisper it's not going badly. I should make more of this free time, this unhurried tempo of attention. You give me hundreds of splendid days, and I return you so few. Yet those I do return pay such a gorgeous dividend that common sense should make me return many more. Had I the slightest bit of brains at all, I'd make sure we had a regular Sabbath.

7

Parenting

Creativity Again

MUCH OF THE work in many marriages goes into parenting, so often it helps to look at parenting freshly. In our view, such a try would do well to thrust a paw in the direction of creativity. As soon as we are willing to take a fresh angle, not jump right into the same old rut, we raise the possibility of becoming creative, coming up with fresh combinations. One of the most consoling angles the theologian can provide sets creativity at the very center of parenting. Just as the biological fertility of the two spouses creates a new physical being, so the psychological and theological creativity of the two spouses can create the conditions for a healthy new personality. Of course, the new little organism itself will have a great say in this process, as even very new parents soon realize. But the process is interactive, far from wholly determined by the little one's innards. If we wish, we can view the entire development of a child as an evolution of meaning in which we've been invited to play a crucial role.

The child is concerned with developing a self and a world in which to be it. By the processes of differentiation and inclusion that we noted above, the child slowly moves through stages of independence and new needs, autonomies and fresh reliances. The middle child, sovereignly cool, may seem less needy than either the gawky teen or the gurgling babe. But the fact of the matter may be that she needs her grant of freedom, depends on being supported in her cool, as much as they need their more obvious helps. Even the best parents grow confused at nature's subtleties, yet they seem instinctively to hew to the same bottom line. That is, they define the reality they see, say the yes or no they find appropriate, but leave open their offspring's path so that he or she can define the reality differently.

Psychologists are much better at telling us how to ease the pains of this process than how to find out where we are going. Their technique of getting us to hear our own voice leads to better accident reports than visions. Accidents and visions relate, of course, and one can't blame psychologists for being leery of the latter. The visions that picture God handing down a map are seldom good signs of health, while the ones that tell Peter or Mary who they ought to become seem almost entirely subjective. When the psychologist or counselor is the parent, the stakes rise considerably. Sensible parents neither force their child to a particular vision nor deny that they themselves view things in certain definite ways (for example, in terms of their Christian faith). By instinct, some of the most faithful parents we know stress trying to be honest. Almost in desperation, they feel that honesty at least lies in their own hands while "objective wisdom" is impossible. They know that at some stages children don't want parents to be confused, aren't ready for that degree of humanity. But over the long haul the parents we've most admired have done their best to describe reality to their children directly as they've felt it to be.

The creativity we find in this honesty is the possibility of broadening the marital adventure. If the two who aspire to become one flesh extend themselves into children, why can they not invite their children along for large parts of their marital journey? As the children develop the capacity to receive it, they might hear an almost formal invitation to come aboard. Then the goals of the couple in work and play, faith and service, could become a family policy. Probably many more families accomplish at least some portion of the substance of this invitation than articulate it clearly. However, probably many fewer children get a sense of their family's overall project than could or should be the case.

One positive example of such an invitation given and received is growing handsomely in our neighborhood. For a family down the block, a great deal of home life focuses on education. The two boys are quite gifted and the parents both prize learning. So a goodly amount of the work the family does explicitly targets the boys' schooling. For example, when a summer enrichment program many states away came to the family's notice, they drew together and worked out a way to bear the financial and psychological expenses of the older boy's attending. When study time became a problem and television was diagnosed as the culprit, out went the family set. To be sure, these values currently are more the parents' than the boys, and down the road may lie some stretches of backlash. But to date, the parents have explained themselves without preaching and the kids have stayed docile without becoming spineless. At its center, the family has fashioned an enterprise upon which all agree and focus. The kids are flattered that their well-being so clearly is important. The parents don't deprive themselves but they do work to take satisfaction in what enhances the minds of their kids. This is not a case of a viciously vicarious satisfaction (the parents are both confident professionals). It is a case of love creating a way to set the family as a whole into an absorbing and rewarding set of collaborations.

No doubt people more experienced than we may at this point want to leap in with dozens of qualifications. Our agenda is not to make family circles into Montessori labs or to beat the drum for pushing one's children. In the case we described, and others we could add, the parents second more than they initiate. For instance, seeing that Alicia is musical, Rich and Nancy give her all possible encouragement, put considerable family resources and time at the service of her musicality. Mark and Brian show other interests so they get other underwritings. But the family considers all five members' interests matter of common cause, so it creates many seasons of growth, time after time of development.

Responsibility

When the creative juices of parenting are flowing, the care and feeding of offspring seems the grandest of vocations. Many natural instincts grow sleek and take wing, for both females and males. The responsibility one has assumed feels right, fitting, generative. It obviously is making one solid, weighty, a person of heft. In religious terms, these are feelings of "consolation," the Spirit putting power to one's sails. Consolation greatly aids the virtue of hope, showing us how things would be, will be, in Christ's kingdom. The only caveat the spiritual masters put forward is that we not grow forgetful of our weakness. All human beings suffer ups and downs, at least touches of mania and depression. So wise human beings don't let themselves get so carried away by consolation that they forget the possibility of desolation (the negative moods). What is up usually comes down, and those who can't anticipate coming down are the ones most likely to crash.

In a brilliant novel of parent-child relations, Robb Forman Dew has captured the desolations that can put the unwary parent into a deep funk. Dinah Howell, a mother of three in her midthirties, unwisely leaves her husband back East each summer and drags her tribe to the small midwestern town she grew up in, where the ghosts of her own childhood complicate her parenting terribly. By midsummer her renewed irritations at her own parents, and the lassitude induced by the relentless heat, have stripped away her maternal confidence. The smallest responsibilities rise up like mountains; getting through breakfast can seem a marathon:

> She settled the children at the table and served them the coffee cake and the eggs she had scrambled, and then she turned to wash up the bowls and pans at the sink while she

took occasional sips of her coffee. When she turned around she saw that Toby had left his place and was not in the kitchen, and that he hadn't eaten at all or drunk any milk. She started up the back stairs to find him and bring him back. To tell him in a voice like God's own that if he didn't eat his eggs and drink his milk he wouldn't get strong, he wouldn't stay well. He had to take her at her word that she knew these things. But she found him at the top of the stairs at the landing, folding up on himself, and when he looked up at her she saw that tears were sliding down his face. And sorrow overtook her; he was such a wiry, pathetic bundle huddled there on the floor. She sat down on the step below him and held him in a hug

"What's the matter, Toby?" she asked, but not without a certain wariness.

And, in fact, he said, "I *hate* eggs, Mama! You know I hate eggs. I didn't want any, but you gave them to me."

It was left to her to decide if this was an accusation—she had served him the eggs—or simply an explanation. "Well, for God's sake, Toby, don't eat them, then."

He put his head down on his knees and didn't move. She and Toby had these battles too often lately, and their warfare had left her vulnerable. She tried to coerce him. "There's your favorite coffee cake. The butter crunch topping. I don't care if you eat your eggs or not, sweetie. I just put them on your plate without thinking. Come on down with me." She won this much by retreating down the stairs, her back turned to him, so that he would have to follow if he expected further concessions. He did follow her and resume his place at the table . . .

When she looked up, she saw that Toby had removed, with surgical precision, all the eggs from his plate and carefully deposited them on his napkin. He had done this, she supposed, so that they could in no way sully his coffee cake. But the steam from his eggs had condensed all around them so that the napkin was a soggy rag, and she knew he had achieved a small victory. She cleared up the table in a silence they all knew, and children very wisely dispersed and played together with remarkable and uncommon good nature. She was sure they knew how deeply she begrudged them these triumphs.[1]

By summer's end Dinah is almost clinically depressed, barely able to drag herself out of bed in the morning. She is fighting so many battles—with her parents, her memories of girlhood, her different self-images, her willful kids—that she is emotionally exhausted. The responsibility for three independent human lives would wipe her out, were she to face it directly, so she shunts it aside with fits of daydreaming. Back East her husband putters at his work, half missing the family and half enjoying an unwonted peace. He wanders into an affair of such low intensity that it seems like sleepwalking, clearly because he has nothing better to do. Robb Forman Dew may not have intended any theological implications, but readers like ourselves find them leaping off the page. When individuals have no religious (ultimate) meaning in their lives, no passion for God, they have little with which to anchor their families. They either flee from their parental responsibilities into the great range of distractions that make surburbia a caricature, or they risk profound depressions. Children whom God does not help us carry, in whose upbringing the Spirit does not console us, easily become oppressive burdens, little enemies whom we begrudge the smallest triumph. That parental love is strong, both inside the churches and outside, testifies to God's universal grace.

Faith

At the end of Dinah Howell's saga, a perspective of faith does open. Where once the succession of trials and crises constituting her family life seemed unrelievedly oppressive, a shift of personality makes it possible to believe that God comes in humble moments, is the deep side of even ordinary frustrations. Such a belief does not make daily banalities into miracles. It does not ease every pain or tear. But it does attack the hopelessness that is so enervating, the feeling deep in our bones that none of it finally matters. In the midst of their parental trials, spouses can indeed wonder whether any of what they do finally matters. The peer pressures on teenagers can seem so much

stronger than the influence of a mother or father that
"What's the use?" echoes late at night in many master
bedrooms. Usually both parents don't fall into this mood
at the same time, so one is able to keep humor and
perspective. But ever since a good friend, one of the
sanest women we know, confessed that she had called the
police because she was afraid she would physically abuse
her middle teenager, we've tried not to underestimate
parental trauma.

In the sober mood this effort has induced, the legendary
parents (especially mothers) of large families have swollen
to almost saintly proportions. The black mother of a huge
flock, frequently abandoned by her husband and almost
always poor, willing her way through day after day by
relying wholeheartedly on Jesus, becomes a most moving
story. Who could know the troubles she's seen? Glory!
Glory, hallelujah![2] The closest parallel in our own experience is a friend who raised ten children, the last born
when she was forty-eight, and in addition carried the
burdens of an abusive husband and a sickly mother. For
most of thirty years she coped with a family growing larger
and larger, and a marriage growing worse and worse, by
the sheer force of a rock-solid faith.

Our friend's marriage has been a disaster, by any canons
we would feel comfortable employing. What love there
was between her husband and herself at the beginning has
been cold perhaps twenty years. In other circumstances,
as she herself would quickly admit, she would have been
well advised to divorce him. While others might have
chosen differently, her own personal view of her obliga-
tions to her children made that seem a faithless option,
the greater of the two evils. So she stayed, learning to live
from day to day. She became efficient, serene, and relentless, digging down to resources she'd never even guessed
she owned. Chief among these was a hunger for God, a
need as real as her need of food or sleep. She began going
to church early each morning, using the quiet familiarity
with the service to focus her heartbreak and helplessness.

Quickly she found herself emerging quite consoled, ready
to face the day's problems. The Christian mysteries went
down so deeply into human pain, looked the ultimate
problems so directly in the face, that they spoke eloquently
to her own situation. From the cross Christ said that God
knows the troubles we've seen. Seated at the right hand of
the Father, he said that all would be well: he had overcome the world.

These were not specific, factual answers. They did not
say, "Tell your husband this, give your number two son
that." What they said, in a wordless, global impression on
her heart, was something like, "You can do it. My grace is
sufficient. Take one day at a time. Enough for this day is
this day's evil. You're not alone. I know what it is costing
you. I ask only that you do the best you can. That will be
enough, believe me. Let go of your anxiety. Cast all those
things that are out of your hands onto my lap. You don't
have to try to run the whole world. In due time you'll see
what it all means, what it is I've been fashioning. Nothing
can separate you from my love."

When people are really up against it, and they contend
with God from naked need, they see the true proportions
of all situations. None of us can add a cubit to our height.
None of us is certain of living tomorrow. All of our lives
rest in the hands of God. If God did not number each of
our hairs, the life of any of us would be hopeless. Faith, in
other words, only needs to become serious for a few hours
and we realize that God asks all of us for *carte blanche*.
When we gather our wits about us, we realize that
everyone's future is shrouded, the only sane gesture is to
sign the blank check and promise we shall try to keep
going. God asks that we try to keep going, not that we
understand it, or like it, or succeed. God asks that we try
to let our lives be what they have always been: gifts, utter
gratuities. As the great believer Teresa of Avila put it: "Let
nothing bother you. Let nothing dismay you. Everything
passes. Patience gains all. God alone is enough."

Detachment

Among psychologists studying child-raising that has gone awry, one school currently getting much attention stresses the failure to discipline effectively. For want of clear guidelines and crisp enforcement, many children grow up confused, undisciplined, aggressive, and well on the way to becoming social, even criminal, problems. The Oregon Social Learning Center in Eugene, Oregon, has tried to develop ways of teaching parents both the woeful effects of their poor discipline and positive strategies for taming their kids:

> The failure of parents to use reasonable reinforcements contingent on steadily monitored behavior places the child in a situation in which he comes to understand that he cannot control by his own actions what happens to him. When one receives penalties unconnected to one's own behavior, one experiences a kind of stress that Martin E. Seligman has called "learned helplessness," just as when one receives rewards that are unearned, one develops "learned laziness."
>
> The treatment at the Learning Center was to teach these troubled parents how to set clear rules, monitor behavior, and make rewards contingent on good behavior and punishment contingent on bad behavior. By rewards, the therapists meant not necessarily giving presents in exchange for some major instance of good conduct but routinely responding in pleasant and supportive ways, or with "points" exchangeable for small privileges (such as ice cream for dessert), to pleasant language and helpful behavior. And by punishment they meant not only assessing major penalties for major misdemeanors but promptly and consistently penalizing unpleasant and destructive language and conduct. An especially favored penalty, the value of which was established by repeated trials, was "time out"—that is, being sent briefly, usually for five minutes, into seclusion in another room, usually the bathroom, without recriminations or long lectures.[3]

The author of the article from which we quote is interested in modifying the behavior of unruly children because unruly children tend to become unruly (criminal) citizens, and criminals are the object of his professional concern as a professor of government at Harvard University. We authors of this book are interested in the discipline of children, and the other subtopics we treat, because it bears on the arduous yet noble project of becoming one flesh in Christian marriage. Without at all wanting to neglect the welfare of children who are not getting the discipline (and so the upbringing) that they deserve, our greater interest is helping Christian spouses see their parenting, as the other aspects of their marital vocation, in the light of grace, the splendid set of offers and powers God lays before them.

In the light of grace, the wisdoms of the Learning Center do not shrink but swell, for the love prompted by the Spirit is reasonable and orderly, firm as well as warm. As both the clinicians at the Learning Center and the author of the article point out, millions of parents manage to discipline their children quite well, doing instinctively what those who lack parental "competence" have painfully to be taught. Instinctively, millions know they must set limits, be consistent, give their children constant feedback, break the patterns of unacceptable behavior by blowing the whistle and announcing, "Time out!" It helps any parent, however, to have such an instinctive wisdom articulated, and it should help Christian parents to have it correlated with their faith.

Parents who love their children and trust in a good Creator may begin by assuming that their children are manageable. God would not build such precious machines without putting in steering mechanisms and governors. True, children have to learn how their machinery works and how to flow into the traffic of other machines, but this is something most manage quite well. So while there are times when parents must give kids special doses of warmth or attention, a lot of the day-by-day business of parenting is just keeping things flowing smoothly.

Now, things flow smoothly when we are free to move

easily, don't get bogged down, are not so attached to fears or hopes that they paralyze us. In the case of child control, the experts suggest moving quickly and lightly. Any significant behavior, good or bad, should get a prompt and crisp response. A word of praise or a correction, a smile or a frown, should feed into a consistent pattern of monitoring. This need not be intrusive or oppressive, let alone nagging or syrupy. It can be as blunt as a terrible two or as subtle as a Byzantine teen.

And, above all, it can be detached: done without a lot of hoopla, expressed almost as naturally and simply as breathing. Fathers don't have to frown, harrumph, and deliver moralistic sermons. Mothers don't have to flutter or snipe. A smile, a wink, a few words can show one knows quite well what is happening and approves, praises, or wants it cut off at the pass. Usually that is enough to get the traffic back under control.

Detachment, then, largely appears as dexterity, lightness, no big deal. In its depths, however, it is a product of the *carte blanche* we've described, a species of holy abandonment. Thus the mother of ten who has shown us such faith is a crisp, no-nonsense householder. Like a maestro at the podium, she nods, draws out, hushes, and beats time, orchestrating round after round of meals and deals into the music of a family centered on God's mystery, awed by God's overwhelming love.

Altruism

The capital phrase that summarizes the Christian understanding of altruism is Jesus' "as yourself." In making a second commandment, like to the first great commandment about loving God completely, Jesus proposed the most radical social theory or politics that has yet challenged the human heart. So root-going, in fact, is this social theory that most of Jesus' followers shy away from facing it. They know that it is going to measure them and find them wanting, so they do their best to keep their acquaintance with it merely notional. Our political systems, economic systems, educational systems, health-care systems, and the rest would all be up for a complete renovation were "as yourself" taken seriously. Some good features of the present systems would be invited out for bows and applause they seldom receive, but more dark features of the present systems would be dragged out into the light, which would make a large number of people very uncomfortable. To consider one's neighbor as another self, and put his or her welfare on a par with one's own, brings a stunning revelation. For those with hearts wide enough to bear it, it implies a God really as good as Jesus, a church worthy of being Christ's body and spouse.

When we search for Jesus' second commandment at the United Nations or on Capitol Hill, we mainly come home discouraged. When we search for it in ordinary households, between parents and children struggling to do right, we come back somewhat encouraged, suspecting once again that the Creator has crafted better than we had been realizing. For between parents and children there does flow something approaching the love of Jesus' second commandment. Many parents do put the welfare of their children on a par with their own, would give their blood for their little one's smile. And it may be that such parents do not hear it read out from the pulpit as often as they should that God sees this sacrificial and wholehearted love, works some wonderful effects through it, and blesses with rich rewards those who forward salvation history by generating it.

In the salad days of doctrinal theology, when giants such as Augustine roamed the Western mind rooting out boulders and planting vast forests, "original sin" became a hot property. It never caught on in the East as it did in the West, nor among Thomists as it did with Augustinians, but it has been a most influential concept. Freed of Augustine's biblical literalism, and of his tendency to tie it to the act of procreation, original sin lately has been flourishing under the banner of "the sin of the world."

With this phrase reconstructionist theologians have been emphasizing the prior context of disorder, warping, "tilt" that all human beings enter. To be born is to be born into an imperfect, unjust, slanted social order. There are the rich and the poor in their indefensible ratios, to the warping of both social classes. There are the gougings caused by sex, race, age, or nationality, irrespective of personal merits. Today, in their rush to get ready for unthinkable wars, the nations divert precious resources from crippled children to nuclear warheads, as silent and sleek as the serpent. In their drive to advance their selfish lifestyles, the Northern nations press tire tracks into the economies and psyches of the Southern nations. All of this is "the sin of the world," the huge machine running amok with no one even close to the controls.

What is God's antidote to the "sin of the world"? By both traditional and contemporary consensus, it is the love that took Christ to his cross. Greater love no one has than this, to lay down life for his friends. In token of the power of this love, the Father raised Jesus from the dead. Jesus' love, the resurrection sings, was stronger than all the sinful hate of his enemies. Between the love of Jesus and the hate of Satan there was no parity. Suffering Satan's hate, taking it into himself, Jesus was wracked by feverish pains. His love was so much stronger, however, that in three days he had done away with Satan's toxins. The faith, hope, and love injected by the Spirit into Jesus' faithful followers now glaze our vessels against both Satan and the sin of the world. Though our bodies are still forfeit to dark forces, our spirits partake of the immortal divine nature (and our bodies one day will also). Dying, Christ destroyed our death and defanged the sin of the world. Rising, he restored our life and made suffering-love the ultimate energy.

All of which has what to do with parenting? Often, a very great deal. For parents are some of life's most prodigal self-spenders, some of the most generous suffering-lovers around. When Isaiah used the figure of a nursing mother to guarantee God's fidelity to Israel (Isa. 49:14–15), he drew on common human experience. The vast majority of nursing mothers would never abandon their children, nor the vast majority of fathers who walk the nursery at night. And though our instinctive loves of an infant shift and take on nuance as our children grow up, in most parents' hearts they always keep beating. So the father of the bride wipes away a tear because he remembers the tiny nose and minuscular nails that first peeked out of the blanket. The mother of the barrister sees him frown and gets a crazy flashback to his hatred of turnips. Despite all their failings and inadequacies, father and mother have spent the best years of their lives helping bride and barrister thrive. Quite beyond their judgment or awareness, they have put into the world, through the small circle they could shape, God's antidote to original sin. Like the benefactors surprised at the judgment scene of Matthew 25, they have a pleasant revelation coming.

8

Prayer

Peace and Quiet

IN TURNING OVER various aspects of the marital relationship—romance, commitment, work, and parenting— we have been doing what theologians are condemned to do, reflecting in search of faith's fuller understanding. The basic tool we have for orienting ourselves in the world, getting on top of our experience, is our capacity for reflection. Informed by Christian tradition and warmed by the love of the Spirit, this capacity can open us to the treasuries of Christian wisdom, ripen in us the specifically Christian ways of loving life in the face of death. But, as any who have gone in search of it know, theological reflection has its conditions. It does not flourish in front of "Saturday Night Live," is not prominent at the local disco. To step back from the rush of one's experience, see the patterns and compare them with Christian counsel, one must hie away to a place of peace and quiet. So libraries offer secluded carrels and post signs saying "Shhhhhhh!" So homes designate certain rooms "studies," congratulating themselves that heavy thinking has thereby been underwritten. Reflection flourishes only in quiet. Theology is never far from silence.

The relation between reflection and prayer is such that one could write these observations in scarlet. If it is true that one needs peace and quiet to study well, get to the shape of things, it is doubly true that one needs quiet to attend to the Spirit, give God material to mold. The first lesson people wanting to pray seriously usually need is a

lesson in "recollection." Unless they are quite atypical
Americans, they begin with parts of themselves scattered
hither and yon. One part is over at the bank, anxiously
watching the computer printouts. Another part is at Life-
Labs, awaiting the results of Sally's biopsy. A frivolous
part daydreams about Saturday's golf game, itching to get
to use the new driver. A deeper part fights the melancho-
lia of fatigue and aging, as fifty steadily draws nigh. To
give God a whole partner for discussion, we need to beat
the triangle and call in these parts. Lumbering back from
different acres of our psyche, they finally squat together at
the campfire and tell us the Lord's sustenance can begin.

Among the prime treasures of a Christian lifestyle,
therefore, is a chance for recollection, peace, and quiet.
Spouses desirous of enhancing the quality of their prayer
would do well to look in this direction. For example, how
goes it now with the later evening, when the kids have
finally bedded down? Do we really get anything from the
television we watch, more than a patch of dubious
distraction? Perhaps we'd be better served by quiet music
and a good book, both taken lightly, with no compulsion to
get through a certain number of sonatas or chapters. In
this way, what the Medievals called *lectio divina*, spiritual
reading, could be usefully rehabilitated today.

Take a good book, whether explicitly religious or simply
artful, and partner it to quiet. Read until it takes hold of
your mind or starts to stir your feelings. Then let it fall
into your lap and go with the thoughts or feelings it has
raised. You will be a rare reader if these thoughts or
feelings don't reflect your deeper preoccupations (of which
you may not have been much aware). Art forms such as
records or books are like Rorschach blots: their meaning is
largely in the eye or ear of the beholder. What a Beetho-
ven quartet does for you in the fall may be much more
impressive than what it does in the spring. What *The
Color Purple* or *Ah, But Your Land Is Beautiful* does
when you are being abused makes it barely the same book
you read last year, when things were going swimmingly.

So it is with thoughts specifically marital, feelings about your love life. When you take the stimulus of a piece of art into a receptive quiet, it will stop being banal, start to reveal its proper weight and mystery. As it does, you will find matter for most profitable converse with God, stuff well worth turning over. That is what prayer does: turns the stuff we now are over to God, the mystery holding our meaning. Physical pain or emotional pain, nagging worries or sudden lifts—all are little semaphores, flares sent up by the unconscious. When they have a full, dark heaven against which to array themselves, they become arresting fireworks. We're never sure precisely what they mean, but we sense that gazing at their passage, and then appreciating the immense space that is their backdrop, is somehow good for our spirits. The two great wonders that preoccupied Immanuel Kant were the starry heavens above and the moral law within. In quiet nights of contemplation, many humble religious seekers have felt them correlate.

For the poet Dante Alighieri, the heavens were much more than just physical objects and forces. Looking to the roof of the world, he felt "the love that moves the stars." This love was God, the Creator of all that is. In the perspective of the stars, the medieval world found order. There is no good reason why our contemporary world could not also find order in the perspective of the stars. For the basic insight on the way to order is the realization that we human beings are simply not the measure. In the peace and quiet of late nights, after slow music or lovely lines, the stars offer alternate measures. Eye has not seen nor ear heard the outreach of such music. How much greater must the outreach of the love that makes it be?

Openness to God

In peace and quiet, we have the chance to drop many of the barriers that we normally erect against God. Part of us hates erecting these barriers, of course, since part of us knows we have been made for God. But a foolish, cowardly, and often more influential part intuits that we cannot deal well with God except honestly, will have to talk turkey if we take on a truly religious contract. So this cowardly part urges more distraction, preoccupation, even false sense of unworthiness ("Who are we to think of heavy intimacy with God?"). All the while, the better part watches ironically, amazed at what fools these mortals choose to be. Although God has on occasion filled us with indescribable peace, we still fear that surrender to God will cost us our freedom. Although we know that independence apart from God isn't worth a chili bean, we hold back, wanting to remain our own person. *Oi vey* what nebbishes.

Mary Gordon's interesting novel *The Company of Women* describes Felicitas Taylor, the young heroine, as bred away from openness to God. Because of her peculiar upbringing in the midst of a circle of devout older women, and her strict tutoring by the priest Father Cyprian, she thinks God cannot be emotionally appealing:

> I cannot talk about God. Of all of them, I alone have no spiritual life. It is Cyprian's fault; he trained me too well, trained me against the sentimental, the susceptibility of the heart. So I will not accept the blandishments of the religious life; I will not look to God for comfort, for succor, or for sweetness. God will have to meet me on the high ground of reason, and there He's a poor contender.
>
> I am interested in the perception of the sacred. So many humans seem to hunger for it: the clear, the unencumbered. I too hunger, but my hunger is specific. If I could see the face of God as free from all necessity, the vision as the reward of a grueling search, the soul stripped down, rock hard, then I would look for Him. The pure light that enlightens every man. If He would show Himself so, then I would seek Him. But I will not let Him into my heart. My daughter is there, my mother, Leo, Cyprian, the women whom I love. I will not open my heart to God. If He is the only God I could worship, He will value my chastity. But I will not be violated; I will not submit myself. I will wait. But I will wait for light, not love.[1]

What is one to make of this strange mixture of religious yearning and rigorous condition-setting? First, that it probably is a good rendering of the psychology of early adulthood, when the demands of honest intellectualism first make themselves forcefully heard. This is the time of absolutes, iconoclasms, anti-idolatry. It is the time when the Protestant principle that would honor the sovereignty of only the true God gets written in hoarfrost, when the Ultimate is no fire, all ice. Felicitas wants God, but only as the First Principle, the Eternal Reason, the Compeller of the Mind. She has yet to learn that the mind is never long compelled by Reason, that the heart has reasons the mind knows not.

God can, of course, compete quite well on the high ground of reason, if reason be understood as the full faculty that the Greeks, the Medievals, the Buddhists, the Hindus, and most other traditional peoples found it to be. It is only the modern West that has thinned reason to a pale gruel, narrowed its scope and cast out its First and Final Cause. For traditional reason God is the Beginning and the Beyond. Human beings only have light because of the inreach of God, only move toward the light because of the divine drawing.[2]

Second, until Felicitas (or we) can accept God's chosen way of coming, the way of incarnate love, there will be no resolution to the puzzle at the center of things, no easing of the central frustration. The human person is a unity, not a dualism of mind and heart. We only find quiet by turning our nearly infinite capacity (to imagine, conceive, yearn) to God to be filled on God's terms. God's terms are grace, goodness almost too great to be believed. Felicitas is right to fear sentimentality but wrong to equate sentimentality with Christian love. So simple a move as gazing at the crucifix could have corrected her of that misapprehension. In due time, when her own preoccupations have shifted from preserving her chastity to bearing fruit, the pains of her daughter, her mother, her husband, and the women she loves will force her to contend with the Whole. Then she will grow grateful that God does not hold her to her youthful rigidity, forces her to grow out toward the place where reason stammers to a stop, quiet becomes eloquence.

God is before us and behind. God is the light luring our minds and the love keeping our hearts. There is no decent project we can pursue that God does not second and deepen. There is no honest or pure emotion we can have that God does not accept. Whether we wish it or not, God is greater than we—in being, goodness, extent. We never know where we came from, where we are going, how to map the whole. So the conditions of our progress, our prayer, our marital growth are always conditions we do not set. Once we have become responsible, we must unlearn our sufficiency. Once it has grown competent, we must surrender our mind. If we cling to our theology, it will become our jailor. If we keep fleeing from God, we will run ourselves down. "Close the doors" (against distraction), Lao Tzu said. "Open your heart to the Way." "Behold, I stand at the door and knock," Revelation has Christ say (Rev. 3:20). If we open we may find eyes like a flame of fire, a voice like the sound of many waters.

Praying Together

One prudent way to try to assure openness to God is to assign oneself a regular time period for prayer. This will not guarantee that the barriers will come down but it will keep setting one to the task. If spouses agree to observe a regular prayer period *together* they probably double their chances of openness. The moral support of the other increases the likelihood that we will show up, and the occasional sharing of the prayer's matter and dynamics renews the faith-commitment at the heart of the marriage. Let us therefore describe how spouses might go about sharing prayer on a regular basis.

One couple we know who have been praying regularly for quite a few years have a daily prayer period of shared silence. Since early morning, right after rising, is the time they find most practical and congenial, they have made praying then as regular as showering and breakfasting. Being together in the silence seems to deepen it. As though they were validating the scriptural text about two or three gathering in Christ's name, more often than not their quiet becomes pregnant, supportive, recentering. Usually the periods of silence have the form of a meditation on, or simple saturation with, the biblical word. Reexamining a text, they let it sink to their depths, feed their hearts, retune their imaginations.

Several times a week, however, they give their prayer a more sacramental format. On the sacramental days they usually adapt the Lord's Supper, taking bread and wine and sharing some liturgical readings. Now and then they add a musical prelude (from a record) or close with a celebrational tune. More frequently they content themselves with a quiet beginning prayer, some silence, a scriptural text, more silence (or discussion, if one feels enlightened), and then a memorial of Jesus' last meal with his friends, when he gave himself to be our food. They pray the Lord's Prayer and share a kiss of peace. They consume the bread and wine and give themselves time to commune with the God who would nourish them. At the end they usually feel they have once again joined their little family church to the great church that never ceases offering the eucharist. Often they make love after this sacramental celebration, to embody the shared faith and life that the memorial of Jesus' sharing has quickened.

Another couple we know try to share a leisurely walk each evening after supper. They live near the ocean and are fascinated by its endless variations. Sometimes they read a scriptural text before they leave, give it time to sink in, and then discuss its implications for themselves as they watch the sun go down or the moon rise up. Other times they just gaze out at the God being revealed in nature, contemplating the beauty and vastness without word or thought, from the simple center of themselves.

This sort of prayer amounts to a shared appreciation of the gift of life, the bounty of God in placing them in a natural world of such beauty, a country of so many advantages and blessings. On the way home they'll talk about their children, now well grown. They'll remember how they used to struggle, before they made a serious commitment to Christ, so they'll renew their appreciation to the Father for the faith they now share. Through the seasons, they watch the waters dazzle with sunshine, go gray with a storm, be swirled by the wind and whipped to a frothy foam. The tides work on their spirits, slowing their anxieties, regulating their breaths. They stamp back into their kitchen, shake off the damp, and enjoy a cup of hot tea. Once more the day has settled into order. Once more they can arrange it in columns, tally it, and make return to the Father of Lights.

Other spouses we know share prayer times with their whole family, extending grace before meals with scriptural readings, decorating Advent or Lenten symbols, having occasional rites of penance and forgiveness. Usually such ceremonies set aside space for family members to speak out their personal thoughts, problems, or suggestions. The focus stays on God, but the actual people present are not neglected. These people know that we must be reconciled to our brother or sister or spouse if our gift is going to lie on the altar fittingly. We must give voice to the pain in our heart, if the others are going to pray for us with full understanding. In their private prayer sessions, when they are alone as a couple, Christian spouses should remember these dynamics, making one of their regular topics for discussion their own relation as a couple. This does not mean they should confuse prayer with self-criticism or become absorbed with themselves. It just means they should try to make their prayer wholly honest, really their own, a word cutting to *their* joint and marrow.

A final form of prayer that we can recommend applies one's senses and imagination to a piece of religious art. Take a favorite portrait of Christ. Place yourself before it as a couple, either physically (if you have a reproduction) or in your mind's eye. Notice the eyes, how they are sad or burning. Hear how the voice would sound. Consider the touch of this man, what the beloved disciple felt as he lay across his breast. Smell the smoke of the fire on which the fish would later bake along the shore. Taste the goodness of this Lord, as you might have after touching his cheek with your lips in farewell. Join hands and share your simple love of him, your regrets for all your failings, your promises to do better, the warmth and joy that well up.

Fruits to Look For

The principal fruits by which serious Christians can discern the Spirit's operations within them are peace and joy. Those who pray regularly and generously may hope, even expect, to harvest these inestimable gifts. That does not mean, of course, a trouble-free life. The peace and joy that the Spirit furnishes undercut this-worldly troubles but hardly eliminate them. Despite real sorrows and afflictions, however, the faithful, prayerful person usually can find serenity and the power to keep affirming life. This is because the dispositions worked in us by regular, serious prayer lead to the substantial fulfillment of our personalities. Prayer of the maturing Christian sort opens us out to the mystery of God, which is the ultimate reality on which our hearts have been set. The light that would fulfill our mind, the love that would fulfill our affections, and the sense of inclusion or connection that would fulfill our differentiated individualities all are available in regular encounter with the real God. In what a famous English mystical text, *The Cloud of Unknowing*, describes as a congenial darkness or opaqueness, we come to deal with God, the Infinite, directly, holistically, through a wordless language of love that is a flow from heart to heart.[3]

What can such peace and joy mean for Christian spouses? The possibilities are too numerous to count, but we can indicate the sorts of benefits. First, there is the basic satisfaction with life, with one's situation, with one's self that prayer in the Spirit creates. Without making us prideful or self-satisfied in the sense of complacent, the fruits of the Spirit of prayer give us contentment, a freedom from turmoil or dissatisfaction. True, there are holy discontents, and they can target both personal holiness and social justice. God can move us to want stronger love, regret our moral ugliness, hunger and thirst for the redress of the widow and the orphan. Out of such feelings the saints have proclaimed themselves the worst sinners and the prophets have lashed out at the godlessness of their times. But these holy discontents do not make people cynical, unable to work, a negative factor in their family or the community. As Paul made clear in discussing the different spiritual gifts, they all subserve the upbuilding of the common body and the common good (1 Cor. 12–14). Our God is not a God of chaos but of order.

So, second, the fruits of prayer lead on to good love and good work, the signs of health we saw previously. To love one must have some positive images of oneself, some sources of warmth, care, and reciprocity. To work one must be free of crippling agitations, able to concentrate and summon up creative imagery. The works of love are the most beautiful, because love is the energy of life and creativity, the force that makes a face glisten, gives luster to a smile. If one is right with God, reconciled to the mystery that defines one on every side, one can put up with the trials of love (spousal, parental, or communitarian). There is "give" in one's psyche, elasticity, so one can bend. Humor comes fairly easily—the gentle, detoxifying kind. Perspective also comes fairly easily, for each day one faces the oceanic Origin, the term that relativizes all else. A traditional liturgical phrase captured much of this: "God, to serve whom is to reign...." Led out from prayer in peace and joy, we are as humble rulers, free beings subject to no tyranny of conscience.

Between two prayerful spouses, these and other good effects of the primal peace and joy can only multiply blessings. The happiness of a good Christian marriage, in fact, is little more than sharing this peace and joy. The sourness of frustrated, crabbed spouses often is the direct result of their not being peaceful at heart, not finding joy at the center. God can give peace and joy unexpectedly, as a bolt from the blue, but the more usual way is for peace and joy to accrue slowly, as the fruit of a regular immersion in prayer. Like the sweet waters that steadily trickle into a fresh pond, the Spirit seeps into our spirits, cleanses and vivifies. Then we have less and less to hide from one another, more and more to reveal. The love of God working to center our hearts pulls like gravity on our love of our spouse, drawing it over toward concentricity. Then we sense a bit of what truly holy people experience intensely and constantly: the presence of God in all things. Then all of our loves inch toward flowing out from and back to the central love that we most directly nourish in prayer.

Thoughts such as these, which follow in the tracks of both our (authors') personal experiences and our studies in prayer, lead us to think that the religious medicine most desperately needed in most places is a strong dose of deep, simple prayer. Again and again, the unhappiness, spite, tension, and frustration that we see swirling around beg healing from the opening of deep prayer. Like poisons welled up in stopped basins, these negative forces would largely run off to the purifying leeching beds, were those suffering them to open up and confess to a real God. Aside from the truly ill, who need professional psychiatric help, legions of the "normally" depressed suffer almost needlessly. They need only find quiet and openness for their raveled sleeves to reknit, their embattled spirits to rest, their souls to find order under the consoling aspect of eternity. But they cannot or will not or do not know how, so Jesus must weep for them as he wept over Jerusalem, the "City of Peace" that ignored the meaning of its own name.

Cheerful Doggedness

For those who can agree to it in good conscience, we recommend applying the *carte blanche* mentioned above to the practice of regular prayer. By this we mean simply deciding that we will show up each day, make an effort to pray, without often questioning its worthwhileness. The Christian tradition, from New Testament times on, is unanimous in witnessing to the superlative value of prayer. If we would accept this and work out a way that we could pray each day, we would give our faith a specific focus. Then, in good times and bad, we would know that we were at least trying to share life with the One pious Jews call the "Master of the Universe," pious Muslims address as "Lord of the Worlds." Whatever came down the pike we could refer to the One who finally controls all the patterns. Like Abraham, we could haggle for good causes. Like Job, we could pour out our complaints. And like both of them, we probably would find our prayers answered somewhat paradoxically. At times we might wear God down, like the widow with the unjust judge (Luke 18: 1–8). At other times we might find our preconceptions turned over, as "thy will be done" took hold. It would be a thoroughgoing religious education, this daily sharing of life with God, and it is as near, as easy, as practicable as fifteen minutes of trying each day.

In such trying, the best attitude to assume or face to give one's *carte blanche* might be a dogged cheerfulness. The dogged side implies showing up, refusing to become discouraged, letting the Spirit teach us how faith is not vision, how the spiritual life leads into what John of the Cross called "dark nights" of the senses and the soul. We must learn that God is not a thing, not a being, far from someone we can manipulate. We must learn that our spontaneous instincts, while not sinful, are self-centered, somewhat childish, quite unrealistic. Reality is the infinity and complete priority of God, as witnessed by the distance of the far galaxies, the profusion of the biological species, the unexpectable form that redemption took in the career of Jesus the Christ. We don't set the rules, create the lines, call the shots in this master play. We have only bit parts, supporting roles, and we're blessed indeed to get them. Until we come to grips with the way faith says things are—theocentric rather than egocentric—we are toddlers in the spiritual life. Since growing up can be painful, we need to make our determination dogged, settle in with a will to stay the course.

The balancing side is good cheer, almost lightness of heart. God is not the grim personage depicted in the Calvinist discourses on double predestination, the rock-face carved above hell. There is too much play in the universe to make this credible, too many otters, hummingbirds, and kids. True enough, Jesus does not come through as a gay blade. The things he saw and the things he suffered made him a man of sorrow—despised, rejected, acquainted with grief. But one can see him smiling at the children, as he dismissed the disciples who would have kept them away (Matt. 19:13–15). One can see him shaking his head at Zacchaeus up in the tree, wondering just how bizarre things were going to get (Luke 19:1–5). John, if not Jesus, is amused as he tells us the story of the man born blind, who makes such dolts of the Pharisees (John 9:13–38). When Jesus draws in the sand, waiting for the one who is without sin and so could cast the first stone, he may well have a glint in his eye, a tug at the corner of his mouth (John 8:2–11). The Old Testament, such a witty and ironic book, couldn't have spawned a completely grim messiah. Jesus came from an earthy, realistic people, well aware of the pratfalls awaiting anyone who puffs himself up toward God. So we do well to make ourselves cheerful before God, jugglers and unprofitable servants. We should not be foolish or silly, but seeing the ironies and taking ourselves lightly will go a long way to helping us persevere at prayer.

God wants us to stay, open up, let the Spirit work our purification. If we were already pure, we'd be in heaven, singing completely on key. As long as we sing somewhat off key, don't have all of our life in order, we have a claim on God the Paraclete. The Paraclete's job is to wash what is soiled, water what is arid, make our deepest prayer, with sighs too deep for words, where God cries out to God. Our job, as the Johannine literature makes plain, is to abide: hold fast, stay open, let ourselves be loved, set our marriages wholly in God's hands, with no thought of moving from either the Spirit or one another. Dogged and cheerful, we—even we—can become spouses who bring one another the fuller love made possible by the Spirit of prayer.

CHAPTER

9

Wisdom

The Long View

FOR SPOUSES WHO cling to the revelation of Jesus Christ as the interpretational key by which they turn the tumblers of experience, the long view is the view of grace. The short view, which daily pressures incline all of us to take, is the view of sin: disorders, disappointments, dislocations. This came home to us once during a visit to New York City. Returning to our hotel room each day grimy and harassed, we would fall into a ritual chant: "What a horrible place! The streets are filthy. The people are nasty. The cabdrivers would as soon mow you down as let you live. How much longer do we have to stay here?" We knew, of course, that this was unfair. We'd been entertained in immaculate apartments, been rendered most gracious service, had two efficient and uneventful cab rides. But a few jostlings and disagreeable experiences, combined with a pace more intense than what we were used to in the Midwest, made us zero in on the negative features, the few things that had rubbed us raw. It was only early one morning, when we were talking after prayer, that we found ourselves marveling at all the things that had to go right for a city of eight million people to function. The phones that worked, the subways that ran, the food that arrived, the heat that arrived, the hospitals that healed and all the rest must have outnumbered the dysfunctions ten to one.

Sometimes we need the same jolt to see accurately the system of events that constitutes our personal lives. Consider,

for instance, the way we can get down on our bodies. Let
a cold sweep into our nose and bones and we begin
planning our retirement. Let a trace of blood taint the
toilet bowl and we start thinking about cancer. To mock
this is not to minimize the fragility of our bodies or to
deny that we are bound to feel a little desolate when
contemplating a possible illness. It is simply to emphasize,
or exaggerate, our tendency to forget all the things that
are functioning smoothly in our bodies, even as we reach
for our handkerchief. Our heart pumps, our blood flows,
our lungs breathe, our enzymes do their stuff. Electrical
charges keep us sensing and thinking. Even while taking
aspirin we get bright ideas. This mortal coil, for all its
escapeless finitude, is an utterly amazing creation. The
more scientists investigate the human body, the more
intricate and mysterious they find it. What indeed are
men and women, that God should have made us little less
than the angels—and given us megamolecules and poly-
peptides in the bargain?

Concerning the long view of the moral order, where we
are concerned with the overall meaning of history, faith
bids us be similarly sanguine. It is true that concise
overviews of world history, such as Toynbee's *Mankind
and Mother Earth,*[1] seem to feature more wars than times
of prosperity or peace. It is true that our current spending
of world resources, which puts far more toward destruc-
tive weapons than education and health care, offers little
reason for dancing. But the gigantic processes of cosmic
and earthly history, or evolution on the universal and
planetary scales, force us somewhat to bracket our pessimism.
Creation, life, and humanity have survived and continued
to evolve for more years than we can significantly imagine.
On a universal clock of one year, human history would
occupy less than a day, the Christian era less than an hour.
In the vast (but ultimately only adequate) framework of
these bigger histories, who is to say that sin has abounded
over grace, death has triumphed over life? The light still

shines in the darkness. One Solzhenitsyn faces down the entire Soviet nation. The darkness still does not comprehend the light. There is as much a mystery to the light (goodness, love) as there is to the darkness (evil, hate). So when Jesus bids us take courage, be not afraid (Matt. 28:10), he has data, as well as personal beauty, on his side. When Paul says that where sin abounded grace abounded the more (Rom. 5:20), he has allies among what we've seen as well as what we've hoped.

The applications to an individual marriage are smaller scale but analogous. If the ten-year mark can bring a terrifying suspicion that somehow we've wandered into a marathon, the forty-year mark can be a time of easy striding, when some of the necessity ("It was necessary for the Christ to suffer and to rise from the dead" [Acts 17:3]) in our early frustrations, fights, confusions, and tears now has become evident. Most of us start as quite callow youths, bright-eyed and generous but naive and self-centered. We expect an exemption from humanity's general draft into disappointment, frustration, membership among the average. We know about the bell-shaped curve, but we think that we somehow will fall out at one of the elite extremes. It takes time for us to learn otherwise, become fitted to a history we little manage. Years go by before we can honestly say character means as much as beauty, peace is more precious than wealth.

The gratitude so prominent in many of the long-married is the appreciation they offer one another for years of patience and endurance. In different ways, each has suffered from the other, as each has made the other wait while he or she grew up. Yet by the time they've climbed the rise that puts their homecoming in sight, these scars seem almost badges of merit. They've brought the couple through at least the fundamental lessons, the primer of maturity. In God's view, they may be taking the couple into a limitless future, a growth that never will stop.

Suffering

Wisdom comes through suffering, the Greek tragedian Aeschylus said, and little before or after him in history has mounted a serious challenge to his saying. We don't know the proportions of human existence until we have descended the depths, seen the black blood of evil and death. We don't glimpse the revolution in Christ's cause until we've gazed at the cross unavertingly. The cross puts up a cautionary hand, stopping our foolish assumption that God must be as soft as we. The depths force us, like the psalmist, to cry out to God for real help, go far beyond social sanction. Two people who have suffered life's blows together are wedded as the untested can never be. Two people who have shared pain and doubt can come to death reconciled.

Still, death is a bitter teacher. From the early Mesopotamian epic of the tragic hero Gilgamesh to the best-seller by the rabbi who ponders why bad things happen to good people,[2] reflective humanity has brooded over death's hold, implicitly petitioning a resurrection. But a resurrection is hard to believe, so most of our tribe become confused or angry at God. As the heavens are above the earth, so God's ways are above our ways. Realizing this personally, as a truth eating at one's own flesh, can make faith and theology riveting. Thus a woman invited into a seminar on what it meant to confess Christian faith today turned the group on its ear by introducing herself with the sentence, "I recently learned that I have terminal cancer."

The seminar went on to publish a book, and the woman's arresting situation kept it from wandering afield. Early in the book appears the rest of the woman's opening statement:

> I had encountered such crises [as terminal cancer] at second hand many times in the characters of English literature, but now I was no longer teaching about crisis. I was face up against my own. In the same hospital room with me was a woman, a black lady who had had both legs

amputated. When her bandages were changed, the pain was excruciating and she cried out. The nurse said to her, "Put your faith in the Lord." The woman replied, "When you do that, you get hit," and then asked me, "Do you have faith in the Lord?" "Well, yes," I replied. "So do I," she said, "but do you like the Lord?" "No," I confessed, "I do not like the Lord." "I don't either. God's not our kind of folks."[3]

When things go wrong, it does seem that God's not our kind of folks. The people who've been good to us would never order up cancer (or divorce or joblessness or...). When we look at our own children, we know we would cut off a hand before we'd let them suffer destructively. So the sufferings that we can make no sense of, that seem but wanton cruelty, test our faith in God, make us doubt we want to have anything to do with such a Being. We assume that when we can see no meaning there is no meaning. Giving God *carte blanche* is more than we can bear. This is natural, human, something all of us should expect from the mirror. It is what Jesus entertained in begging that the cup of suffering might pass from him. The difference between Jesus and us is the immediacy with which Jesus added, "Nevertheless not my will, but thine, be done" (Luke 22:42).

Once we counseled a young woman through a painful divorce. As far as we could tell, since we had come on the scene after the couple had separated, she was almost completely the innocent, injured party. Her husband had had a string of affairs and finally decided he wanted a newer, sleeker model. She had two beautiful children and the sort of concussion that comes from a huge clout to an unsuspecting, undefended psyche. The woman had resources—training as a nurse, joy in motherhood, striking good looks—but while she was staggering from this blow these resources gave her no confidence she would recover. Instinctively she turned for support to the faith in which she had been raised. To that point in her life faith had been but part of the landscape: familiar, comfortable, but hardly preoccupying. In the new depths of experience to which she had been thrust, it suddenly became powerful. The woman had no head of theology, so it was not her faith's concepts that consoled her. It was her perception that a community wanted to care for the wounded like herself because it was a community called together by a healer.

Christians make a community called together by a healer. Most of us only appreciate the significance and splendor of this fact when we find ourselves limping. This is true for the marital dimension of our faith as much as any other. God's forgiveness and healing are as germane to our marital sins and illnesses as to our sins in business or our illnesses of private faith. When we begin to see the selfishnesses, bad tempers, envies, infidelities, and other viruses of our marriages as things faith reaches out to heal, we begin to appreciate the therapies God has provided our human condition. And then, with such an appreciation, we may reset some of our questions about death, the hardest aspect of our human condition.

That we die may be a mercy, for otherwise we might be kept out of a genuine fulfillment. When we die is mysterious; who can say what would be the best hour? We want to live, and are healthy for this wanting, but the One who made us says we must die. "What does God know?" we are tempted to ask, and then we may remember Christ's cross. He knows everything, and from the inside, the way a victim knows evil, a person reviled knows shame. Yet, *because* he knows it this way, he has become power and wisdom: "We preach Christ crucified, a stumbling block to Jews and folly to Gentiles, but to those who are called, both Jews and Greeks, Christ the power of God and the wisdom of God. For the foolishness of God is wiser than men, and the weakness of God is stronger than men" (1 Cor. 1:23–25). God's solution to the problem of suffering is grace we never could conceive, love that makes a completely new creation.

Jesus

For Eastern Christianity, Jesus is principally the icon of the Father enfleshed. He is the basic sacrament or physical form in which the divine love has pitched its tent in our world.[4] For Western Christianity Jesus is primarily the redeemer or savior from sin. Both of these motifs merge in the eucharist, where Christ gives himself to nourish in us a life stronger than death. The classical New Testament text comes from John 6, where Jesus is disputing with skeptical fellow Jews:

> "I am the bread of life. Your fathers ate the manna in the wilderness, and they died. This is the bread which comes down from heaven, that a man may eat of it and not die. I am the living bread which came down from heaven; if any one eats of this bread, he will live for ever; and the bread which I shall give for the life of the world is my flesh." The Jews then disputed among themselves, saying, "How can this man give us his flesh to eat?" So Jesus said to them, "Truly, truly, I say to you, unless you eat the flesh of the Son of man and drink his blood, you have no life in you; he who eats my flesh and drinks my blood has eternal life, and I will raise him up at the last day. For my flesh is food indeed, and my blood is drink indeed. He who eats my flesh and drinks my blood abides in me, and I in him. As the living Father sent me, and I live because of the Father, so he who eats me will live because of me. This is the bread which came down from heaven, not such as the fathers ate and died; he who eats this bread will live for ever."
>
> —John 6:48–58

Christians who ponder the scriptures and meet Jesus there do well and nourish their souls. Christians who frequent the sacraments and meet Jesus there also do well and also nourish their souls. When a scriptural text such as John 6 is joined to a sacramental reception of Jesus, one has the fullest of meetings and nourishments. The Jesus who walked the shores of Galilee and discoursed as John presents him steps from the page and becomes the living

Lord, present in his church, one with his bride and body. In giving himself to be the food and drink of his faithful, he promises that the divine life he has from the Father will become their life, raising them into the immortality of the Father, Son, and Spirit.

The sacrifice on the cross that the eucharist memorializes works both the forgiveness of sins and the bestowal of divine life. One of Charles Wesley's *Hymns on the Lord's Supper* captures both motifs:

> Jesu, dear, redeeming Lord,
> Magnify thy Dying word;
> In thy ordinance appear,
> Come, and meet thy followers here.
>
> In the rite thou hast enjoin'd
> Let us now our Savior find,
> Drink thy blood for sinners shed,
> Taste thee in the broken bread.
>
> Thou our faithful hearts prepare,
> Thou thy pardoning grace declare;
> Thou that hast for sinners died,
> Show thyself the Crucified.
>
> All the power of sin remove,
> Fill us with thy perfect love,
> Stamp us with the stamp Divine,
> Seal our souls forever thine.[5]

The sacramental Christ is a "medicine of immortality," the church fathers used to say. Could he not be for us at least a strong aid in marital suffering? Psychologically, many Christians experience a sense of refreshment, nurture, and healing in their receptions of Christ. In one act, they find forgiveness of sins (healing grace) and strengthening of divine life (elevating grace). The peace and joy of the Spirit return. They are minded to make a new beginning. What (ontological) changes occur in their being, lie out of sight, must be taken on faith. The traditional faith, however, is that we *are* changed by our receptions of the sacraments, do emerge different in our being. It is not that we take divinity into ourselves, as a metabolism in which the inferior breaks down the superior. It is that divinity takes us into itself, making us partners of the divine nature (2 Pet. 1:4).

Jesus, then, lives in and with us. We live, now not just ourselves, but Christ lives in us. However difficult the conception, the claim of faith is indisputable. The same Lord who died and rose for our salvation and justification is the bread of life, God's food for the life of the world. Spouses do well to partake of this food, sacramentalize their lives, regularly stir up their faith in the resurrection. Along with their experience of the Spirit, their experience of the eucharistic Lord is a down payment on the heavenly life they can hope to share, must believe in as part of the orthodox creed. Apart from a lively faith in this heavenly life, their marriages lack the full vision necessary for Christian wisdom.

The message of the gospel makes no full sense without the dimension of the resurrection. The proportions of the Christian program are lost if we try to jam it into this-worldly containers. As Paul saw, if we live for this world only, we are of all people the most to be pitied (1 Cor. 15:19). If we have not come to grips with the mighty immortality of the God from whom Eastern Christianity begs mercy, we have yet to understand our calling. Death may part spouses, as the wedding formula acknowledges, but faith says they will not remain in the grave but rise. There may be no marrying in heaven, as the strange text in Matthew 22:30 proclaims, but if real, historical people are resurrected, all their relationships, most certainly including the one in which they have lost their separateness to become one flesh, will be preserved and fulfilled. What the Johannine Christ promises under the symbols of bread and wine, flesh and blood, makes the power and wisdom of God palpable, palatable, food for not only thought but mind-boggling hope.

Sacramentality

As an incarnational and eucharistic religion, Christianity celebrates God's materialization. That the Word became flesh and dwelt among us is the axis of our faith. We do not need to flee the world to find our God. However much prayer, suffering, and love have their other-worldly dimensions, they never denigrate this world, allow us to call our flesh bad. The effect of these basic Christian dispositions is an outlook, a wisdom, that is thoroughly sacramental or iconic. When Christians look at a situation or a person, the Spirit of their faith invites them to see it in symbolic terms. Beyond what the situation or person may convey in strictly literal terms lies the possibility of richer overtones, deeper implications. A third dimension longs to swell out, to rescue the situation from the sterility of a flatland. The lines of Christ begin to shade in, to paint the person as a member of Christ's body. We have to keep this sort of imagination in check, of course, lest we lose hold on ordinary, daily reality. But in proper degree it is the work of the enlivening Spirit, who would make the world appear as scriptural faith says it is: full of grace and truth.

The yields of a sacramental sensitivity for marriage are direct and numerous. Marriage is a many-leveled process of communication. The exact, denotative meanings we convey (the patches of questions and answers) are but a tiny portion of our exchanges. So spouses become famous for being able to read one another's moods instantly, the smallest quiver of the lip or tightening of the jaw speaking volumes. Each day a kiss on the cheek or a pat on the backside crosses chasms. The indirectnesses of many women dance intriguing duets with the directnesses of many men. The metaphor of sexual sharing grows more and more freighted. If God was a prodigal architect in planning the heavens, God was a brilliant poet in designing the human species. Living at the hinge of matter and spirit, we must read all our insights in phantasms, project all our meanings in material forms. Were we reflective about this necessity, we might appreciate why God "had" to have the Word take flesh, how fitting it was that God's good news was poured into healings and stories, dyings and risings.

Take a man and a woman sitting in a car prior to going in to a prayer meeting. They are locked in serious talk, not fighting but not just passing pleasantries. Probably they are again discussing their teenage children, their usual concern recently. When the prayer meeting comes to the time for sharing concerns, the couple explain the problem they been having with the telephone. Neither time limits nor fines have worked to make the children keep the line open. So they are considering a second phone, for which the children would pay, or the service that warns when another call is incoming. Both of these options offend the mother, who doesn't think they should be necessary. The father simply wants the line cleared. They make light of the problem (encouraged by other people's recitals of similar problems), but their laughter is rueful, their capitulation reluctant. Others who are paying attention know the problem is not settled. The couple have yet to agree on what they should do, so the children will probably continue to manipulate them.

How is it that even spectators to an interaction like this can sense dozens of implications, while the couple themselves may hesitate to bring the matter up at all, so convinced are they that it is "loaded"? The more sensitive we are to what may be at stake in a given situation, the more layers of implication we provide for. Suppose, then, that spouses tried to attune themselves to the grace-implications at stake in a given situation. What layers useful to faith might they not suspect? We don't mean to gild every little encounter with mystical glitter. Youngsters in the spiritual life who see in every fall tree a burning bush give sensitivity a tedious name. The same with those awkward importers of sensitivity jargon, who can make "special person" a reason for grinding one's teeth. No, all we have in mind is a sober but active summons of faith that opens us to the Spirit, lets the religious dimensions of a situation emerge should God choose.

In the great phone chase that we described, there may not be extraordinary meanings. Probably what is going on in the children is only par for the contemporary teenage course. What is going on between the parents may be more significant, since this is something they have yet to work out. If his instinct is to get a second phone and stick it to the kids to pay for it, she has to try to hear the "justice" he is pursuing. If her instinct is to resist more consumption, he has to try to feel her hunger for a stripped, uncluttered, religiously free lifestyle. Neither instinct is right or wrong in any heavy, absolute way. Either could develop a workable solution. But how they understand the overtones of their interaction, whether they keep the conflicts down and the complementarities on the rise, is a stiff little test. Were he to let her instinct work within him, giving it docile quiet in which to make its pitch, they might bring the whole family to discuss the problem thoroughly, deepening the sensitivity of all parties to the grains of faith. Then the marriage would take another piddling, apparently insignificant bit of flesh and open it to the Spirit. Then another patch of shared life would be sacramentalized.

Bread Broken and Joy Shared

The foolishness of God, wiser than humans, and the weakness of God, stronger than humans, invite us to be converted and believe in the good news that earth might be fair, all her children wise. When our closures are broken open, our selfishnesses turned around, the goodness of creation can shine forth in dazzling colors, rainbows and Florida sunsets. The long view of a God always at the beginning and the beyond, always full of better purposes than we can descry, turns out to sacramentalize the short view, the little fourscore of years in which we strut our stuff. What comparative religionists discuss in terms of the polarity between transcendence and immanence compacts most densely, marries most beautifully, in the Word become flesh. The God who is utterly other (transcendent) becomes absolutely near (immanent). After Jesus of Nazareth nothing lacks the touch of God, is not part of the personal play through which God is ordering the universe. After Jesus of Nazareth there is no completely profane space or time, everything is graced. What Teilhard de Chardin called "Christogenesis" is the buildup of the body of Christ at the center of evolution (biogenesis, noegenesis). In every patch of meaning, the Word that expresses the total divine meaning flashes forth, gives off a glimmer of itself.

One senses this humbly but most consolingly around the family table. The bread that we break, does it not convey the care of the Lord? The joy that we share, is it not a portent of the messianic banquet, when the King who brings God's peace will bid all his followers feast? True, these biblical figures beg translation today, when our world's storage bins soon will have to feed five billions. Nonetheless, wherever people enjoy bread and wine, rice and fish, the care of our parental God hovers. In all the interactions among God's children, God the parent hopes for a sharing, a support, a mutual allegiance, a show of human solidarity that would make the world able to believe in God's love.

With sacramental wisdom, God has put his own credibility, as well as the fate of the earth, into the hands of his children. The two go together, as do the two great commands. The sign of our loving God with whole mind, heart, soul, and strength is how we treat our neighbors, day by day, near and far. Similarly, God's providential guidance of history goes together with our human freedom and responsibility. Standing outside of time, God need not be the competitor of our freedom, a puppeteer controlling us by strings we cannot see. For God to have chosen a providential design and human beings to have freely worked it out are coincident propositions. God's choosing of something does not occur "before" our enacting of it. There is no before and after in God. So what is, after the fact, on our worldly level, exists as having been, in God's timeless eternity, part of the overall creational plan that God chooses for coordinating all creatures' actions.

To be sure, this is a classical theological problem, and those who find little illumination in it, or little spiritual profit from it, need not trouble themselves. Our point in alluding to it is simply that our sacramental situations need not always be looking over their shoulders, wondering whether God's interpretation of them is something completely different than their instinctive own. By the title of providence, as well as the titles of incarnation and grace, we can believe that our breakings of bread and sharings of joy bear us divine love straightforwardly. God is not devious, trifling with our emotions. There may be further dimensions we shall only grasp in the future but we can trust what we enjoy right now.

We place some emphasis on this confidence in creation that faith solicits because we find its lack (doubt, suspicion, timidity) mottling so many human situations, constricting so many marriages. The couple we alluded to previously who suffered so much trauma coming to grips with his midlife affair were both crippled by a doubting, suspicious view of their spaces and times. If they had a flash of joy or delight or desire, they tended to suspect it. If they had a preference or personal stake in a decision they thought they had to lean over backwards against that option. This might have been bearable, had they had special gifts of self-knowledge and humor, but their being both unreflective and earnest made it a disastrous package. By the time his frustrations broke out, they were completely at sea, in need of a full emotional reeducation. The world that had come from the hands of their God and been blessed with the historical presence of their Christ was murky, foreign, and uncongenial, especially in their own sexuality. They did not know the meaning of grace's having abounded over sin, Luther's "sin bravely."

The wisdom we need as Christian spouses and parents is a love of mortal life that would send us forth in peace, with courage, holding on to what is good. It would have us return no one evil for evil. It would empower us to strengthen the fainthearted, support the weak, help the suffering, honor all people, love and serve our Lord, rejoicing in the power of his Holy Spirit, anointed with the blessing of Father, Son, and Comforter. Cleansing our eyes, quickening our love, it would infuse our homes, dinner tables, nurseries, workshops, bedrooms, and playgrounds with grace, worthy of the Word who took flesh and pitched his tent in our midst.

10

Summary

For This Reason

FOR REASON OF marriage, children leave fathers and mothers. Grown, at least in body, they cling to one another and become one flesh. The sexual union they achieve becomes a metaphor for the complete sharing of intention, time, and fortune that their marriage presses to achieve. Being together they represent humanity as it was when God coined it in the divine image: male and female, two complementary halves joined to make a whole. One assumes that God has purposes in designing creatures as they come to be. To be human as female and male must have some function and utility. Biologists may hesitate to speak in this way (of teleology), but believers need blush not at all. Of course God designs purposefully, creates wisely. "God" would be a limp concept indeed were it to omit purpose and wisdom. So we are coordinated to one another as men and women in ways both patent and subtle. The vast majority of the population, both now and throughout the ages, have never doubted that humanity was female-male, man and woman made a dyad.

This is not to say, of course, that most societies, historically, have treated the two sexes equally. In terms of both civil and religious rights, women have tended to be second-class citizens.[1] By today's egalitarian standards, the Christian church has done women many disservices, failed to render practical and political the Pauline notion that in Christ there is neither male nor female. While the church fathers never denied the natural orientation of male and female or the God-givenness of marriage, many of them said slurring things about women, because they found female sexuality seductive. When celibacy was the clerical obligation or ideal and the clergy were overwhelmingly male, men's natural sexual orientation toward women became a problem for them. That this was more men's problem than women's didn't occur to the fathers as quickly as it should, so women bore more psychological backlash than they should. Fit to the lineaments of Eve, women heard they were to work out their salvation in childbearing and obedience to their husbands. For that reason, many marriages were less sacramental, friendly, and erotic than they might well have been.

We are fortunate to live in a time when men and women are within striking distance of viewing one another as thorough equals. That women still make on average only sixty-two cents to each male dollar tilts all the sexes' relations, but the confusions brought by women's new aspirations are more than compensated by the chance men and women now have to deal with one another as distinct people rather than stereotypes. Faith can call this a happy chance, God's providential way of helping two who are trying to become one flesh reveal more of themselves and bear richer fruit. If both sexes will fight their temptations to ideology (pursuing abstract ideals rather than responding to concrete people), the playful, delightful interactions that emerge will give further nuance to God's reason for doing the business of procreation heterosexually. Biology students who've watched amoebas reproduce realize it could have been much less interesting.

Sometimes it makes the divine reasons for marriage more gripping to read them out of the development of especially impressive couples. One couple who come to mind at this point are in their midfifties, enjoying the fruits of their hard but successful work in business and starting to delight in the joys of grandparenthood. The man began his business career as a very junior member of an accounting firm and now runs things from the top. This puts him in touch with leading social and political figures, but he shows no desire to become a mover or shaker. The woman has strong interests in art and religion, both of which she has studied at the graduate level. She too came from humble origins, but her natural refinement would make her at home among royalty. What distinguishes this couple from many others who appear similar outwardly (upper-middle class and well-appointed) is their good humor and full sharing. They take themselves lightly, seeing their good fortune—travels, highly placed friends, and objects of art—as unexpected gifts. They are never pompous or pretentious. They do not hoard their wealth but are open-handed to a fault. And the interests or concerns of one are the interests or concerns of the other.

This latter trait is perhaps especially striking in the man, most of whose peers in business might indulge their wives' artistic or religious interests but would not actually share in them. This man, however, shows a full interest, from reading the books his wife recommends to picking her up at the bus station each week after her long jaunt to the distant state university for graduate classes. He taxies to the door the stray people she has collected—panhandlers and Holy Rollers make a beeline for her, as though God has marked the path. He helps her keep perspective when her professor, about the age of her son, turns back her term paper as insufficiently annotated. Before long he has her laughing, the sound that clearly is the music of his life. The couple have been gracious and good to newcomers like us. They have been a model of how to love fine things without becoming possessive, develop a refined taste without becoming self-centered, soft, or forgetful of the billions struggling for bare necessities. For this reason we've often thanked God for their marriage, marveling at their nearly perfect coordination. As so fully his-hers, male-female, their marriage is a rich sacrament.

Flesh of Flesh

From the time of Adam, spouses have been inclined to view one another as flesh of their flesh, the other half of their soul. In the myth of Adam's rib (Gen. 2:21–25), the biblical authors depicted the natural bond between man and woman as though they shared the same bone. Freed of its suggestions of females' subordination, the depiction becomes quite touching. Other peoples have written myths of human origin in similar veins. Thus in the Japanese (Shinto) account Izanagi and Izanami are instructed to fertilize the earth. The woman gazes at the man and says, "Ah, how fair a youth!" The man gazes at the woman and says, "Ah, how fair a maiden!" (The man is upset that the woman broke protocol and spoke first, but that is secondary.)

This initial perception of "fairness," as we have seen, is the erotic impulse that gets marriages going. It becomes Christianized, maturing toward the biblical agape, in the community of affection, the coincidence of concern, that "flesh of my flesh" suggests. Then the good of the other is as important as one's own good. Then forgiving the other is easier than forgiving oneself.

For those with strong instincts of faith, the idealization of the beloved, the almost blind "excess" that romance often shows, reveals a touching aspect of the biblical God:

In the past this perception of the loved one has been criticized, maligned, and ridiculed. It has been said that the lover tries to squeeze the beloved into a preconceived, ideal mold that fulfills the lover's own needs. Rather it seems to us that an inner perceptual process in the passion of romantic love encourages us to magnify all the positive characteristics of our beloved. Critics say this is evidence of illusion, is not objective, and is irrational. But we find Yahweh's comment to Gideon in Paddy Chayefsky's play of that name a better explanation. Yahweh has chosen Gideon, the least important member of the weakest clan in Manasseh, to rescue Israel from the Midianites. Gideon says, "Why me?" Yahweh answers, "Passion has no reason."

Indeed, throughout salvation history Yahweh chooses

people who seem unattractive and powerless. And Jesus continues this in his selection of followers. Why, we wonder, did Yahweh ever pick the ragged band of nomads and bring them out of Egypt? Why didn't Jesus pick the learned and powerful in Israel? Because the creator of love, a passionate lover, knows no reason when it comes to the beloved. Again our experience of romantic love leads us to the Other who is responsible for its existence.[2]

The authors of this reflection, a psychiatrist and a theologian, play up the love of the sexes to illustrate God's passion, as they play up the passion of God to illumine human love and marriage. If God is love, as the New Testament regularly proclaims, human love is our privileged disclosure of God. Among all our experiences it is the one that best reveals what the Father of Jesus Christ is like. The way that we feel toward our beloved is like the way that Christ feels toward the church. The way we would console and support our beloved is like the way the Spirit works as our Paraclete.

If the relation between spouses is "flesh of my flesh," the relation between God and God's beloved might be called "spirit of my spirit." What we are, flesh, is the medium for expressing our communion as man and woman. What God is, spirit, is the medium for expressing the communion of Creator and creature. When Augustine spoke of God as "more intimate to me than I am to myself," he implied this spiritual communion. The depths of the image of God, the human creature, flow into the light and love of the Creator. Spouses who take their love to its depths, communicating from the substance of their souls, root it in the divine lover who is present at the bedrock of each of them.

Without such communion, overlapping of affections and concerns, sense that what we two *are* is essentially the same, marriages quickly slip into discord. The time and place where outsiders realize that a marriage has turned discordant tend to linger long after in their memories, as painful experiences they wish they'd missed. We can still see a luxurious house on Long Island and the remains of a special meal (cherried chicken). A little girl plays in the corner, more nervous than would seem normal. The man sits at one end of the table, speaking of home repairs: electrical circuits, tiling, sprinkler systems. The woman runs back and forth serving, occasionally mentioning her courses at the university, her plans for social work. There is no connection between the ends of the table. The man doesn't lift a finger to help with the meal. The woman realizes that her schooling and career plans, like her cooking, are separate from the work and interests the man thinks center the marriage. The house is huge, far more than the three of them will ever be able to use. In the yard sits a Chris Craft cruiser, with a full stereo system. The man displays all the cruiser's furnishings, every fitting and feature. The woman's face is blank, controlled, the face of a person reluctant to acknowledge something she finds distasteful, painful.

Within six months of this scene we heard that the couple had separated and were in the process of filing for divorce. In the aftermath, that seemed a good decision. Nothing that we had observed, apart from the physical presence of the child, gave any hint that the man and woman were connected. In no way did they suggest "flesh of my flesh," "spirit of my spirit." No God or Christ seemed to symbolize their aspirations or resources for union. No joy and peace put a glow on the cherries or made the conversation sparkle. We came home sad, disappointed, depressed. The compact of Adam and Eve lay shattered. It was only a matter of time before the sharp pieces fell out.

Against Loneliness

When the woman who had prepared cherried chicken left the huge house in which she had been rattling around to search for a new life apart from the man with whom she could never connect, she went back into the pool of lonely people, even more wounded than those who had never had their hopes for marital sharing devastated. The few letters we got from her centered around this theme. The little girl was a great joy and comfort, but the burdens of being a single parent, working, and going to school left the woman bowed low. She had little time for a social life, and what she saw of the singles scene in the city to which she had moved turned her cold. She threw herself into her responsibilities, distracting herself from deeper thoughts that tended to paralyze. But she had the sense of being in a work camp, a drab stretch of the Gulag, waiting for release from an indefinite sentence. Later, about the time that her little girl entered the fourth grade, she met a good man and remarried. For close to five years, though, she was swimming under water, rising toward the surface at only the slightest of angles. Several years after her remarriage she told us:

> It was as though my emotions atrophied, I wasn't using my equipment for joy, sex, or creative homemaking so it withered. Laura [her daughter] gave me someone to love and care for. Otherwise I might have dried up completely. I guess it was three or four years before I realized how badly I'd been burned. I found myself doubting all my instincts and judgments, because I'd made such a bad mistake. I didn't know whether Ken [her first husband] had changed drastically or whether before we married I never saw him as he really was. I wanted to break out of my loneliness but every time I'd meet a man I'd wonder whether he wouldn't turn out (really) to be uncommunicative, not genuinely interested in my side of the relationship. And I started to see the same wariness in other single women over twenty-five, and even to wonder whether some men didn't have it too. Even many of the married people I met kept missing one another, moving on two different planes. Sure, a few had terrific marriages, and I had to admire them for that. In fact, I was grateful for any patch of sunshine. But a great many married people seemed almost as lonely as I was. That was *very* depressing.

It is not good for human beings to be alone, scripture says (Gen. 2:8). The complete image of God depends on our connecting, cooperating, communing. Once people have achieved sufficient identity to be considered past adolescence, they usually search for a love that will set them in the enriching context of an intimate sharing. The meaning of the statistics on this search depends greatly on the interpreter, but given that the ratio of divorces to continuing marriages lately has become about fifty-fifty (for first marriages among people in their twenties and thirties), the meaning quite certainly is that communion is not a sure bet. To break out of negative solitude (there is a positive solitude) requires some skillful moves.

Primarily, one has to be blessed with, or generate, a strong interest in another person, making him or her a beloved, the center of a new common cause. The blessing of eros is that it accomplishes this easily. One is not merely interested in another person, one is fascinated, nearly obsessed. With such a powerful initial thrust, a marriage needs only to keep momentum for the partners' loneliness to be thoroughly tamed. Loneliness may raise its head again in middle age (or any time among the especially reflective), but even then usually it will be a paper tiger, just a temporary face of the always vulnerable human condition.

Against the specter of loneliness, the Spirit gives us dreams of sexual coordination. As hard and soft, direct and oblique, aggressive and receptive—or any other combination of such characteristics, either stereotypic or newly made—men and women find their sharing special, richer than what they can find among just their own kind. The feminist jibe, "A woman without a man is like a fish without a bicycle," makes a useful point (independent identity is good and necessary). Uncomplemented, however, it usually seems harsh and cold. To the women who are with men happily, in ways they must honestly call enriching, it is but a partial insight and one often blinkered by personal pain. The loneliness of men and women who want to be coordinated, connected, yet cannot seem to work this out tells against the saying, making it seem almost flippant, just as the suffocation, or paradoxical loneliness, of men and women who are badly fused tells for it. Either way, it becomes a truth from the battlefield, rather than a truth from a time of peace. If war is the normal condition, truths from the battlefield can be right on the mark. If peace is what we're made for, truths from the battlefield can be disastrously misleading.

Marriage ought to conquer loneliness, squeeze out its poisons. That marriage needs the grace of Christ to accomplish this merely says that marriage works with ordinary human beings who are imperfect and sinful. Better for us to meet our imperfections early, realize our need of God, than slide away into separate silences. Better for us to clash, express our pains, and reconcile in topsy-turvy passion than to fall into patterns of jabbering and saying nothing, withdrawing and putting our feelings in deep freeze. If we wish, marriage can fight a very good fight against loneliness. Unless we wish and work and pray, marriage can show us a deeper loneliness than most of us are ready to handle.

Against Selfishness

W. T. Tyler's bleak but moving novel *The Ants of God* plays in the midspace between loneliness and selfishness. The central character, McDermott, is a mercenary pilot emotionally crippled by a childhood in a dour orphanage and harsh experiences in the Vietnam War. He has learned to rely only on himself and keep his emotions well tamped. Three consecutive sentences are a speech; he lives with silence in stoic comfort. The relations he has with a hippie tourist and a missionary nurse while running guns in Ethiopia suggest the attractions that selflessness starts to have in middle age. The pilot is thirty-seven, the hippie twenty-three, the nurse about thirty-five. Still a pampered child, the hippie is bright but dominated by her emotional needs. She doesn't realize that the man's silence is an affliction, something it would take an earthquake to change. It makes sense that she should ask him to be more outgoing, to give more of himself, but her excessive need cheapens her pleas. Their breakup is less the ruin of a potentially rich love than her rite of passage into adulthood.

The girl has told the man that she is leaving, going away with some Peace Corps volunteers:

> "You're sure you've made up your mind." "I think so." She looked across the field. "I wish you'd told me earlier." "I didn't decide for sure until this morning." "When are you leaving?" "Tomorrow morning. Eight o'clock to Cairo and Athens." She knew he'd be surprised. He stood with his hands on his hips, studying her face, and then the field beyond. "I always knew you would," he said. "I didn't think I'd be surprised either but I am. Tomorrow morning." He shook his head. "That's pretty soon." "I think sometimes you could have made it easier. More part of what you were doing. More of your life." "Yeah. Maybe so." "You never took me on those flights you promised." "I should have, I guess. I always thought there would be time for it"... "Oh, God," she wept miserably, "why is it always me?"[3]

The combination of loneliness and selfishness in this relation virtually condemns it to failure. By contrast, the pilot's relation with the missionary nurse brings him face to face with a silence as deep as his own, but one focused outward on other people's needs. His erotic attraction for her, and hers for him, doesn't fire until they realize that if they would give up their fear of self-revelation they might find a love that could move their strength beyond mere endurance, into a light where they could confront the idiocy in their work and still keep trying.

The man has pinned the woman's arms, to force her to listen to him:

> She turned her face toward him. "What are you talking about?" "You," he said. "Just you. Nobody else. Just you. You're better than any of them. The whole idiot crowd. The UN...Osgood. The Ethiopians. The Sudanese crowd.

Stop thinking you're not. You've done more than any of them could do. Don't you know that? . . . stop fighting and listen to me! No one could have done more—" She watched him stubbornly, her eyes dark. "Are you finished? You're hurting my wrists." "No, I'm not finished." He relaxed his grip, but when she tried to sit up, he held her again. "Did you hear what I said?" She turned her head away and didn't answer. Still they lay on the bed, McDermott holding her arms. Finally she turned her head and looked up at him. "Yes," she said. He lifted himself, still over her. "Okay. Remember that then. You're better than any of them." She stared up at him as he studied her face. "Okay, I'm through then. That's all I wanted to say." He released her wrists and kissed her suddenly on the mouth and stood up.[4]

With this violent breakthrough, both the pilot and the nurse are free to see things more objectively. He has reached out to another person ardently for the first time, making her good his passion. She *must* see how her lack of self-respect is draining off her joy. For her the fight on the bed breaks down what had been nearly a prison. She had been giving of herself to the villagers generously but with no joy, almost masochistically. A subtler selfishness, more defensible than the hippie girl's but none the less injurious, had taken hold in her endurance and closed her inner precincts. The pilot, drawn toward those precincts by the woman's strength of character, became furious at the toll her stoicism was taking. As though she were the alter ego he had long wanted to hold at arm's length and shake, he forced from his viscera a love both tough and open-eyed. By comparison the love possible with the hippie girl became almost trifling.

With experience, we realize that love and selfishness have layer upon layer. Self-discovery in heterosexual relations becomes like peeling an onion. But the institution of marriage, its character as a formal coordination of man and woman, can give this peeling, stripping, or ascesis support and dignity. Growth to the point where we are willing to shake one another physically to win a deeper honesty and love makes the Spirit sigh with satisfaction. Behind ordinary doors, in unremarkable kitchens and bedrooms, many people become powerfully mature. Accepting the Spirit's invitation, braving dark nights to glimpse living flames of love, they do violence to the old man of sin, put on the new mind of Christ. When Augustine spoke of loving God unto contempt of self, he probably meant this sort of maturation.

For God's Purposes

"Everything exits into mystery," an old Christian adage has it. We never see the full scope of what we do, and we are not likely to witness the Parousia. The final judgment at which all will stand revealed is for us a thing of faith, not vision. So we must surrender our marriages, as our whole lives, into God's hands. As time inclines us, we should cede more and more of what has happened to us, what we have become, how we seem shaped, to the leading of the Spirit. This too is faith rather than vision, matter for quiet prayer rather than fussy accounting. God is greater than our hearts, and God knows all. Our hearts always have reasons for condemning us, piles of evils we've done or goods we've left undone. As God made us, and we had no say, so God will judge us, and our say will be but partial. We must trust that Jesus' say is good news, a God of love rather than a God of wrath. We must believe that we have been, are being, will be justified through God's goodness and no merits of our own.

Justification by faith means for marriage not an encouragement of sloppiness but an encouragement of grace and playfulness. When we are not huge in our own eyes, do not have egos that blot out the sun, the world is vast and wonderful, the sun an inexhaustible bounty. In the light of such a sun, the goods of the earth form a cornucopia: the groaning larder of Thanksgiving, the firm flesh of our spouse, the apple cheeks of our children. These are not gifts to be clung to, grasped, stored up as a miser would. Those who store up goods and think they are secure have forgotten the biblical admonition: "Fool! This night your soul is required of you; and the things you have prepared, whose will they be?" (Luke 12:20).

God's purposes for us in our marriages must be gracious. This is the Ariadne's thread to which we can cling. Nothing can separate us from the gracious love of God. If these staples of faith are to take flesh, occupy space in our daily living, they must mean a *carte blanche* from God to us. "Somehow," God is saying, "you will find the strength to accept what happens to you and turn it to religious account. In some way, everything in your life is redeemable, even your own sins." The genius of God's solution to the problems of human life is never clearer than at this point. Christ *has* overcome the world. There is indeed an assured success, an impossibility of failure. If even our own negations of God can be overcome, bought back, rewoven into the tapestry that depicts God's goodness, everything is on our side. If even our sins against one another need not be wholly mortal, our marriages always are graced.

These are perceptions of faith, of course. Only considerable living can blend them with common sense about human beings' likely performances, prudential wisdom about how flawed and badly-willed people probably will move here and now. Although no marriage stands outside God's grace, some marital partners choose to think themselves or their marriages beyond redemption. Their malformations and the seductions of their culture may conspire to make them right, in overt, statistical terms. They may well be headed for the column marked "failure." In few cases, however, will both parties to such a marriage have been believers faithful enough to have relaxed together before God, played and wept in the Spirit's company. Exceptions can occur to any rule, but we suspect that exceptions to this rule are rare. Apart from cases of psychic incompetence, when spouses in effect have no religious freedom, the option of opening to the Spirit stands as God's effective challenge, God's concrete willingness to be tested. We suspect that the human partners to such a test back down far more frequently than they try the silence, cast their bread forth, and find themselves unanswered.

Indirectly, this is true also of single partners to a difficult marriage. Their prayers and generosities alone may not save the marriage, but they can save the self. This, too, we have seen over and over: partners battered and bruised but still floating with their heads above water. The former student of ours who was given his walking papers by his bride of a year is back on his feet now. He staggered for a while, rubbed his head as though hit by a brick, but slowly got his eyes back in focus. The same with the longer-term cases we've already pondered: the mother of ten slugging along year after year, the mother of two traded in for a sleeker model. Their sufferings are things that ought not to be, traces of Christ's crucifixion. In faith, however, their sufferings can become things that somehow had to be, ingredients of God's hidden purposes. Peter's speech in Acts 3 is the classical text on this theme: "And now, brethren, I know that you acted in ignorance, as did also your rulers. But what God foretold by the mouth of all the prophets, that his Christ should suffer, he thus fulfilled" (3:17–18; see also Gen. 45:1–15).

For those whose cups run over, the message remains the same. The ultimate meaning and purposes of good fortune also lie out of our hands. If we prosper in marriage, we remain unprofitable servants. We may plant and water, but only God gives the increase. This is fortune deeper than any material or emotional prospering. For the increases of God are far more certain than any increases our banking can achieve. The future of our marriages is much safer when we place them in God's keeping than when we trust to talents, wisdom, or merits of our own. God gives us *carte blanche* assurances that we mirror the love of Christ for the church so that we can give God back a *carte blanche* availability. So where there is hatred, let us be signs of love. Where there is despair, let us be signs of hope. Where there is division, let us become one flesh.

Notes

Chapter 1

1. See Rosemary Radford Ruether, "Misogynism and Virginal Feminism in the Fathers of the Church," in *Religion and Sexism*, ed. Rosemary Radford Ruether. (New York: Simon & Schuster, 1974), pp. 150–183.
2. See Robert Kegan, *The Evolving Self*. (Cambridge, MA: Harvard University Press, 1982.)
3. Robert Coles, *The Old Ones of New Mexico*. (Albuquerque: University of New Mexico Press, 1973), p. 6.

Chapter 2

1. See Erik Erikson, *The Life Cycle Completed*. (New York: W. W. Norton, 1982.)
2. Huub Oosterhuis, *Your Word Is Near*. (New York: Newman Press, 1968), pp. 64–65.
3. See Carol Gilligan, *In a Different Voice*. (Cambridge, MA: Harvard University Press, 1982.)
4. See Dorothy Dinnerstein, *The Mermaid and the Minotaur*. (New York: Harper & Row, 1976.)

Chapter 3

1. See Jacques Guillet, et al., *Discernment of Spirits*. (Collegeville, MN: The Liturgical Press, 1970.)
2. See John Carmody, *The Progressive Pilgrim*. (Notre Dame, IN: Fides-Claretian, 1980.)

Chapter 4

1. Dick Francis, *Flying Finish*. (New York: Harper & Row, 1966), p. 72.

2. Anne Tyler, *Morgan's Passing*. (New York: Berkeley Books, 1983), pp. 36–37.
3. Sergius Bolshakoff and M. Basil Pennington, *In Search of True Wisdom*. (Garden City, NY: Doubleday, 1979), pp. 60–61.

Chapter 5

1. See Letty A. Russell, *The Future of Partnership*. (Philadelphia: Westminster, 1979.)
2. See William F. Lynch, *Images of Hope*. (New York: Mentor-Omega, 1965.)
3. See Monika K. Hellwig, *Sign of Reconciliation and Conversion*. (Wilmington, DL: Michael Glazier, 1982.)
4. Anne Tyler, *Dinner at the Homesick Restaurant*. (New York: Knopf, 1982), pp. 100–101.

Chapter 6

1. Studs Terkel, *Working*. (New York: Pantheon, 1974), p. xxiv.
2. See Robert Coles, *Privileged Ones*. (Boston: Little, Brown & Co., 1977.)
3. Mark Zborowski and Elizabeth Herzog, *Life Is with People*. (New York: Schocken, 1962.)

Chapter 7

1. Robb Forman Dew, *Dale Loves Sophie to Death*. (New York: Penguin, 1982), pp. 38–40.
2. See Vincent Harding, "Out of the Cauldron of Struggle," *Soundings* CXI, 3 (Fall 1978), pp. 339–354.
3. James Q. Wilson, "Raising Kids," *The Atlantic*, 252/4 (October 1983), pp. 53–54.

Chapter 8

1. Mary Gordon, *The Company of Women*. (New York: Random House, 1980), pp. 264–265.
2. See Eric Voegelin, "Reason: The Classic Experience,"

in his *Anamnesis*. (Notre Dame, IN: University of Notre Dame Press, 1978), pp. 89–115.

3. See William Johnston, ed., *The Cloud of Unknowing*. (Garden City, NY: Image Books, 1973.)

Chapter 9

1. Arnold Toynbee, *Mankind and Mother Earth*. (New York: Oxford University Press, 1976.)
2. Harold S. Kushner, *When Bad Things Happen To Good People*. (New York: Avon Books, 1983.)
3. Patrick Henry and Thomas Stransky, eds., *God on Our Minds*. (Philadelphia: Fortress, 1982), pp. 5–6.
4. See Aidan Nichols, *The Art of God Incarnate*. (New York: Paulist, 1980.)
5. John and Charles Wesley: *Selected Writings and Hymns*, ed. Frank Whaling. (Ramsey, NJ: Paulist, 1981), p. 255. (Hymn 33 in the 1780 *Hymnbook*, absent in the 1933 *Hymnbook*).

Chapter 10

1. See Denise Lardner Carmody, *Women and World Religions*. (Nashville: Abingdon, 1979.)
2. Joan Meyer Anzia and Mary G. Durkin, *Marital Intimacy*. (New York: Andrews and McMeel, 1980), p. 20.
3. W. T. Tyler, *The Ants of God*. (New York: The Dial Press, 1981), pp. 201–202.
4. *Ibid.*, p. 219.

Annotated Bibliography

Anzia, John Meyer and Durkin, Mary G., *Marital Intimacy*. New York: Andrews and McMeel, 1980. A psychiatrist and theologian present a warm, positive view of marital love. Especially good on early romantic peaks and first valleys.

Bailey, Derrick Sherwin, *The Mystery of Love and Marriage*. New York: Harper & Brothers, 1952. A good standard treatment, stressing the main biblical texts, by an Anglican priest.

Barbeau, Clayton C., *Creative Marriage: The Middle Years*. New York: Seabury, 1976. An imaginative and positive approach to problems of fidelity and persistence, by a Christian family counselor.

Barnhouse, Ruth Tiffany and Holmes, Urban T., III, eds., *Male and Female: Christian Approaches to Sexuality*. New York: Seabury, 1976. Psychological, historical, and theological studies by prominent contemporary Christian thinkers.

Bernard, Jessie, *The Future of Marriage*, Second Edition. New Haven: Yale University Press, 1982. A prominent sociologist's influential survey of where the institution of marriage is headed in American culture.

Brill, Earl H., *The Christian Moral Vision*. New York: Seabury, 1979. A good overview of both the personal and social issues in a contemporary Christian ethics.

Brown, Robert McAfee, *Creative Dislocation—The Movement of Grace*. Nashville: Abingdon, 1980. A personal report on progress in Christian faith that lays stress on political and marital aspects.

Carmody, Denise Lardner, *Feminism and Christianity*. Nashville: Abingdon, 1982. A two-way reflection that tries to show complementarities and mutual supplements.

Carmody, John, *Toward a Holistic Spirituality*. Ramsey, NJ: Paulist, 1983. An essay in search of the interconnections among all the major aspects of lay Christian life and their center in God's love.

Dew, Robb Forman, *Dale Loves Sophie to Death*. New York: Penguin, 1982. A sensitive novel of a young wife and mother caught in several webs of confusion and discouragement.

Doherty, Dennis, ed., *Dimensions of Human Sexuality*. Garden City, NY: Doubleday, 1979. Essays dealing with most of the major areas involved in working out a contemporary Christian theology of sex.

Erikson, Erik H., *The Life Cycle Completed*. New York: W. W. Norton, 1982. A summarizing view of typical development through the life cycle by the most honored theoretician.

Fowler, James W., *Stages of Faith*. San Francisco: Harper & Row, 1981. A thorough application of life-cycle theory to the development of faith, featuring many interesting cases.

Gilligan, Carol, *In a Different Voice*. Cambridge, MA: Harvard University Press, 1982. A developmental psychologist's contribution to a feminist view of women's life cycles.

Groome, Thomas H., *Christian Religious Education*. San Francisco: Harper & Row, 1980. A solid reflection on what sharing the Christian story and vision entails.

Haughton, Rosemary, *The Passionate God*. New York: Paulist, 1981. A deep yet readable and moving book about God's love by an outstanding spiritual writer who is the mother of ten.

Henry, Patrick and Stransky, Thomas, eds., *God on Our Minds*. Philadelphia: Fortress, 1982. An ecumenical discussion of what God means in contemporary, experiential terms.

Kasper, Walter, *Theology of Christian Marriage*. New York: Seabury, 1980. A prominent Roman Catholic theologian's reflections on the human values, sacramental dimension, unity, and contemporary status of Christian marriage.

Kegan, Robert, *The Evolving Self*. Cambridge, MA: Harvard University Press, 1982. A creative new look at the processes of human personality development as an ongoing search for deeper meaning.

McGinnis, Kathleen and James, *Parenting for Peace and Justice*. Maryknoll, NY: Orbis, 1981. Good advice on how to educate children in Christian social ideals.

Mackin, Theodore, *What Is Marriage?* Ramsey, NJ: Paulist, 1982. A good historical overview of the Christian theology of marriage.

Nichols, Aidan, *The Art of God Incarnate*. New York: Paulist, 1980. A history of Christian faith's ceaseless artistic efforts to render the Incarnation.

Pearce, Joseph Chilton, *Magical Child*. New York: Bantam, 1980. A stimulating call to rethink child-rearing by a man involved in many new streams of scientific and psychological thought.

Roberts, J. Deotis, *Roots of a Black Future: Family and Church*. Philadelphia: Westminster, 1980. A prominent black theologian and churchman sketches the history and future prospects of what he considers the two key black institutions.

Saliers, Don E., *The Soul in Paraphrase*. New York: Seabury, 1980. A good book by a leading liturgist focused on the religious affections.

Seifert, Harvey, *Explorations in Meditation and Contemplation*. Nashville: The Upper Room, 1981. A solid introduction to the varieties of meditation and contemplation.

Thomas, David M., *Christian Marriage*. Wilmington, DL:

Michael Glazier, 1983. Historical, theological, and spiritual observations, focused on the sacramentality of marriage.

Tyler, Anne, *Dinner at the Homesick Restaurant*. New York: Berkeley Books, 1983. A justly honored novel of family life, especially insightful on mother-child relations.

Updike, John, *Rabbit Is Rich*. New York: Fawcett Crest, 1981. An insightful novel about a mediocre man and a mediocre marriage at middle age that shows love to be as hardy as crabgrass.

Walker, Alice, *The Color Purple*. New York: Washington Square, 1982. A lyric novel of black women's struggles to find dignity, love, and a credible God.

Denise Carmody is Professor of Religion and John Carmody is Adjunct Professor of Religion at Wichita State University, Wichita, Kansas. Mrs. Carmody was awarded a Ph.D. degree from Boston College in Massachusetts. Mr. Carmody received a Ph.D. degree from Stanford University in California.

Both authors have a long list of publishing credits, including *Women & World Religions* and *The Oldest God* by Denise Carmody; and *Ecology and Religion, Reexamining Conscience,* and *Theology for the 1980s* by John Carmody.